June 2007   720.1

The Architecture of Happiness

The Architecture of Happiness
Alain de Botton

PANTHEON BOOKS

New York

All rights reserved. Published in the United States by Pantheon Books,
a division of Random House, Inc., New York. Originally published
in Great Britain by Hamish Hamilton, London.

Pantheon and colophon are registered trademarks of Random House, Inc.

Library of Congress Cataloging-in-Publication Data

De Botton, Alain.
The architecture of happiness / Alain de Botton.
p. cm.
ISBN 0-375-42443-1
1. Architecture—Psychological aspects. 2. Architecture and
society. 3. Architecture—Aesthetics. I. Title.

NA2540.D34 2006   720.1'3—dc22   2006044797

www.pantheonbooks.com

Printed in the United States of America
First American Edition
9 8 7 6 5 4 3

for Charlotte

Contents

I. The Significance of Architecture

1.

A terraced house on a tree-lined street. Earlier today, the house rang with
the sound of children's cries and adult voices, but since the last occupant
took off (with her satchel) a few hours ago, it has been left to sample
the morning by itself. The sun has risen over the gables of the buildings
opposite and now washes through the ground-floor windows, painting the
interior walls a buttery yellow and warming the grainy-red brick façade.
Within shafts of sunlight, platelets of dust move as if in obedience to the
rhythms of a silent waltz. From the hallway, the low murmur of accelerat-
ing traffic can be detected a few blocks away. Occasionally, the letter-box
opens with a rasp to admit a plaintive leaflet.

The house gives signs of enjoying the emptiness. It is rearranging itself
after the night, clearing its pipes and cracking its joints. This dignified and
seasoned creature, with its coppery veins and wooden feet nestled in a
bed of clay, has endured much: balls bounced against its garden flanks,
doors slammed in rage, headstands attempted along its corridors, the
weight and sighs of electrical equipment and the probings of inexperi-
enced plumbers into its innards. A family of four shelters in it, joined by
a colony of ants around the foundations and, in spring time, by broods
of robins in the chimney stack. It also lends a shoulder to a frail (or just
indolent) sweet-pea which leans against the garden wall, indulging the
peripatetic courtship of a circle of bees.

The house has grown into a knowledgeable witness. It has been party to
early seductions, it has watched homework being written, it has observed
swaddled babies freshly arrived from hospital, it has been surprised in
the middle of the night by whispered conferences in the kitchen. It has
experienced winter evenings when its windows were as cold as bags of
frozen peas and midsummer dusks when its brick walls held the warmth
of newly baked bread.

It has provided not only physical but also psychological sanctuary. It has been a guardian of identity. Over the years, its owners have returned from periods away and, on looking around them, remembered who they were. The flagstones on the ground floor speak of serenity and aged grace, while the regularity of the kitchen cabinets offers a model of unintimidating order and discipline. The dining table, with its waxy tablecloth printed with large buttercups, suggests a burst of playfulness which is thrown into relief by a sterner concrete wall nearby. Along the stairs, small still-lives of eggs and lemons draw attention to the intricacy and beauty of everyday things. On a ledge beneath a window, a glass jar of cornflowers helps to resist the pull towards dejection. On the upper floor, a narrow empty room allows space for restorative thoughts to hatch, its skylight giving out onto impatient clouds migrating rapidly over cranes and chimney pots.

Although this house may lack solutions to a great many of its occupants' ills, its rooms nevertheless give evidence of a happiness to which architecture has made its distinctive contribution.

2.

Yet a concern for architecture has never been free from a degree of suspicion. Doubts have been raised about the subject's seriousness, its moral worth and its cost. A thought-provoking number of the world's most intelligent people have disdained any interest in decoration and design, equating contentment with discarnate and invisible matters instead.

The Ancient Greek Stoic philosopher Epictetus is said to have demanded of a heart-broken friend whose house had burnt to the ground, 'If you really understand what governs the universe, how can you yearn for bits of stone and pretty rock?' (It is unclear how much longer the friendship lasted.) Legend recounts that after hearing the voice of God, the Christian hermit Alexandra sold her house, shut herself in a tomb and never looked at the outside world again, while her fellow hermit Paul of Scete slept on a blanket on the floor of a windowless mud hut and recited 300 prayers every day, suffering only when he heard of another holy man who had managed 700 and slept in a coffin.

Such austerity has been a historical constant. In the spring of 1137 the Cistercian monk St Bernard of Clairvaux travelled all the way around Lake Geneva without noticing it was even there. Likewise, after four years in his monastery, St Bernard could not report whether the dining area had a vaulted ceiling (it does) or how many windows there were in the sanctuary of his church (three). On a visit to the Charterhouse of Dauphiné, St Bernard astonished his hosts by arriving on a magnificent white horse diametrically opposed to the ascetic values he professed, but he explained that he had borrowed the animal from a wealthy uncle and had simply failed to register its appearance on a four-day journey across France.

3.

Nevertheless, such determined efforts to scorn visual experience have always been matched by equally persistent attempts to mould the material world to graceful ends. People have strained their backs carving flowers into their roof beams and their eyesight embroidering animals onto their tablecloths. They have given up weekends to hide unsightly cables behind ledges. They have thought carefully about appropriate kitchen work-surfaces. They have imagined living in unattainably expensive houses pictured in magazines and then felt sad, as one does on passing an attractive stranger in a crowded street.

We seem divided between an urge to override our senses and numb ourselves to our settings and a contradictory impulse to acknowledge the extent to which our identities are indelibly connected to, and will shift along with, our locations. An ugly room can coagulate any loose suspicions as to the incompleteness of life, while a sun-lit one set with honey-coloured limestone tiles can lend support to whatever is most hopeful within us.

Belief in the significance of architecture is premised on the notion that we are, for better or for worse, different people in different places – and on the conviction that it is architecture's task to render vivid to us who we might ideally be.

4.

We are sometimes eager to celebrate the influence of our surroundings. In the living room of a house in the Czech Republic, we see an example of how walls, chairs and floors can combine to create an atmosphere in which the best sides of us are offered the opportunity to flourish. We accept with gratitude the power that a single room can possess.

But sensitivity to architecture also has its more problematic aspects. If one room can alter how we feel, if our happiness can hang on the colour of the walls or the shape of a door, what will happen to us in most of the places we are forced to look at and inhabit? What will we experience in a house with prison-like windows, stained carpet tiles and plastic curtains?

It is to prevent the possibility of permanent anguish that we can be led to shut our eyes to most of what is around us, for we are never far from damp stains and cracked ceilings, shattered cities and rusting dockyards. We can't remain sensitive indefinitely to environments which we don't have the means to alter for the good – and end up as conscious as we can afford to be. Echoing the attitude of Stoic philosophers or St Bernard around Lake Geneva, we may find ourselves arguing that, ultimately, it doesn't much matter what buildings look like, what is on the ceiling or how the wall is treated – professions of detachment that stem not so much from an insensitivity to beauty as from a desire to deflect the sadness we would face if we left ourselves open to all of beauty's many absences.

Architecture can render vivid to us who we might ideally be:
Mies van der Rohe, dining area, Tugendhat House, Brno, 1930

5.

There is no shortage of reasons to be suspicious of the ambition to create great architecture. Buildings rarely make palpable the efforts that their construction demands. They are coyly silent about the bankruptcies, the delays, the fear and the dust that they impose. A nonchalant appearance is a frequent feature of their charm. It is only when we try our own hand at construction that we are initiated into the torments associated with persuading materials and other humans to cooperate with our designs, with ensuring that two pieces of glass will be joined in a neat line, that a lamp will hang symmetrically over the stairs, that a boiler will light up when it should or that concrete pillars will marry a roof without complaint.

Even when we have attained our goals, our buildings have a grievous tendency to fall apart again with precipitate speed. It can be hard to walk into a freshly decorated house without feeling pre-emptively sad at the decay impatiently waiting to begin: how soon the walls will crack, the white cupboards will yellow and the carpets stain. The ruins of the Ancient World offer a mocking lesson for anyone waiting for builders to finish their work. How proud the householders of Pompeii must have been.

In his essay 'On Transience' (1916) Sigmund Freud recalled a walk he took in the Dolomite Mountains with the poet Rainer Maria Rilke. It was an exquisite summer's day; the flowers were in bloom and brightly coloured butterflies danced above the meadows. The psychoanalyst was glad to be outdoors (it had been raining all week), but his companion walked with his head bowed, his eyes fixed on the ground, and remained taciturn throughout the excursion. It wasn't that Rilke was oblivious to the beauty around him; he simply could not overlook how impermanent everything was. In Freud's words, he was unable to forget 'that all this beauty was fated to extinction, that it would vanish when winter came, like all human beauty and all the beauty that men have created or may create'.

Freud was unsympathetic; for him, the capacity to love anything attractive, however fragile it might be, was a hallmark of psychological health. But Rilke's stance, though inconvenient, helpfully emphasises how it can be those most in thrall to beauty who will be especially aware of, and saddened by, its ephemeral character. Such melancholic enthusiasts will see the moth hole beneath the curtain swatch and the ruin beneath the plan. They may at the last moment cancel an appointment with an estate agent, having realised that the house under offer, as well as the city and even civilisation itself, will soon enough be reduced to fragments of shattered brick over which cockroaches will triumphantly crawl. They may prefer to rent a room or live in a barrel out of a reluctance to contemplate the slow disintegration of the objects of their love.

At its apex, a passion for architecture may turn us into aesthetes, eccentric figures who must watch over their houses with the vigilance of museum guards, patrolling their rooms in search of stains, a damp cloth or sponge in hand. Aesthetes will have no choice but to forgo the company of small children and, during dinner with friends, will have to ignore the conversation in order to focus on whether someone might lean back and inadvertently leave a head-shaped imprint on the wall.

It would be pleasant to refuse in a muscular spirit to lend stray blemishes genuine significance. However, aesthetes force us to consider whether happiness may not sometimes turn on the presence or absence of a fingerprint, whether in certain situations beauty and ugliness may not lie only a few millimetres apart, whether a single mark might not wreck a wall or an errant brush stroke undo a landscape painting. We should thank these sensitive spirits for pointing us with theatrical honesty towards the possibility of a genuine antithesis between competing values: for example, an attachment to beautiful architecture and the pursuit of an exuberant and affectionate family life.

How wise were the ancient philosophers in suggesting that we exclude from our vision of contentment anything that might one day be covered by lava or blow down in a hurricane, succumb to a chocolate smear or absorb a wine stain.

6.

Architecture is perplexing, too, in how inconsistent is its capacity to generate the happiness on which its claim to our attention is founded. While an attractive building may on occasion flatter an ascending mood, there will be times when the most congenial of locations will be unable to dislodge our sadness or misanthropy.

We can feel anxious and envious even though the floor we're standing on has been imported from a remote quarry, and finely sculpted window frames have been painted a soothing grey. Our inner metronome can be unimpressed by the efforts of workmen to create a fountain or nurture a symmetrical line of oak trees. We can fall into a petty argument which ends in threats of divorce in a building by Geoffrey Bawa or Louis Kahn. Houses can invite us to join them in a mood which we find ourselves incapable of summoning. The noblest architecture can sometimes do less for us than a siesta or an aspirin.

Those who have made architectural beauty their life's work know only too well how futile their efforts can prove. After an exhaustive study of the buildings of Venice, in a moment of depressive lucidity, John Ruskin acknowledged that few Venetians in fact seemed elevated by their city, perhaps the most beautiful urban tapestry in the world. Alongside St Mark's Church (described by Ruskin in *The Stones of Venice* as 'a Book of Common Prayer, a vast illuminated missal, bound with alabaster instead of parchment, studded with porphyry pillars instead of jewels, and written within and without in letters of enamel and gold'), they sat in cafés, read the papers, sunbathed, bickered and stole from one another as, high on the church's roof, unobserved, 'the images of Christ and His angels looked down upon them.'

Endowed with a power that is as unreliable as it often is inexpressible, architecture will always compete poorly with utilitarian demands for humanity's resources. How hard it is to make a case for the cost of tearing down and rebuilding a mean but serviceable street. How awkward to have to defend, in the face of more tangible needs, the benefits of realigning a crooked lamppost or replacing an ill-matched window frame. Beautiful architecture has none of the unambiguous advantages of a vaccine or a bowl of rice. Its construction will hence never be raised to a dominant political priority, for even if the whole of the man-made world could, through relentless effort and sacrifice, be modelled to rival St Mark's Square, even if we could spend the rest of our lives in the Villa Rotonda or the Glass House, we would still often be in a bad mood.

7.

Not only do beautiful houses falter as guarantors of happiness, they can also be accused of failing to improve the characters of those who live in them.

It seems reasonable to suppose that people will possess some of the qualities of the buildings they are drawn to: to expect that if they are alive to the charm of an ancient farmhouse with walls made of irregular chiselled stones set in light mortar, if they can appreciate the play of candlelight against hand-decorated tiles, can be seduced by libraries with shelves filled from floor to ceiling with books that emit a sweet dusty smell and are content to lie on the floor tracing the knotted border of an intricate Turkoman rug, then they will know something about patience and stability, tenderness and sweetness, intelligence and worldliness, scepticism and trust. We expect that such enthusiasts will be committed to infusing their whole lives with the values embodied in the objects of their appreciation.

But, whatever the theoretical affinities between beauty and goodness, it is undeniable that, in practice, farmhouses and lodges, mansions and

We would still often be in a bad mood:
Philip Johnson, The Glass House, New Canaan, Connecticut, 1949

riverside apartments have played host to innumerous tyrants and murderers, sadists and snobs, to characters with a chilling indifference to the disjunctures between the qualities manifested in their surroundings and in their lives.

Medieval devotional paintings may try to remind us of sadness and sin, they may seek to train us away from arrogance and worldly pursuits and render us properly humble before the mysteries and hardships of life, but they will hang in a living room without active protest while butlers circulate the finger food and butchers plot their next move.

Architecture may well possess moral messages; it simply has no power to enforce them. It offers suggestions instead of making laws. It invites, rather than orders, us to emulate its spirit and cannot prevent its own abuse.

We should be kind enough not to blame buildings for our own failure to honour the advice they can only ever subtly proffer.

8.
Suspicion of architecture may in the end be said to centre around the modesty of the claims that can realistically be made on its behalf. Reverence for beautiful buildings does not seem a high ambition on which to pin our hopes for happiness, at least when compared with the results we might associate with untying a scientific knot or falling in love, amassing a fortune or initiating revolution. To care deeply about a field that achieves so little, and yet consumes so many of our resources, forces us to admit to a disturbing, even degrading lack of aspiration.

In its ineffectiveness, architecture shares in the bathos of gardening: an interest in door handles or ceiling mouldings can seem no less worthy of mockery than a concern for the progress of rose or lavender bushes. It is forgivable to conclude that there must be grander causes to which human beings might devote themselves.

However, after coming up against some of the sterner setbacks which

The moral ineffectiveness of a beautiful house:
Hermann Göring (in white) at home with the French Ambassador and, to the right,
Generals Vuillemin and Milch. In the background, *Saints Margarethe and Dorothea*,
German (fifteenth century), and *Lucretia* (1532) by Lucas Cranach

bedevil emotional and political life, we may well arrive at a more chari-
table assessment of the significance of beauty – of islands of perfection,
in which we can find an echo of an ideal which we once hoped to lay
a permanent claim to. Life may have to show itself to us in some of its
authentically tragic colours before we can begin to grow properly visu-
ally responsive to its subtler offerings, whether in the form of a tapestry
or a Corinthian column, a slate tile or a lamp. It tends not to be young
couples in love who stop to admire a weathered brick wall or the descent
of a banister towards a hallway, a disregard for such circumscribed beauty
being a corollary of an optimistic belief in the possibility of attaining a
more visceral, definitive variety of happiness.

We may need to have made an indelible mark on our lives, to have
married the wrong person, pursued an unfulfilling career into middle age
or lost a loved one before architecture can begin to have any perceptible
impact on us, for when we speak of being 'moved' by a building, we allude
to a bitter-sweet feeling of contrast between the noble qualities written
into a structure and the sadder wider reality within which we know them
to exist. A lump rises in our throat at the sight of beauty from an implicit
knowledge that the happiness it hints at is the exception.

In his memoirs, the German theologian Paul Tillich explained that
art had always left him cold as a pampered and trouble-free young man,
despite the best pedagogical efforts of his parents and teachers. Then the
First World War broke out, he was called up and, in a period of leave from
his battalion (three quarters of whose members would be killed in the
course of the conflict), he found himself in the Kaiser Friedrich Museum
in Berlin during a rain storm. There, in a small upper gallery, he came
across Sandro Botticelli's *Madonna and Child with Eight Singing Angels* and,
on meeting the wise, fragile, compassionate gaze of the Virgin, surprised
himself by beginning to sob uncontrollably. He experienced what he
described as a moment of 'revelatory ecstasy', tears welling up in his eyes

Life is not usually like this:
Ken Shuttleworth, Crescent House, Wiltshire, 1997

Sandro Botticelli, *Madonna and Child with Eight Singing Angels*, 1477

at the disjunction between the exceptionally tender atmosphere of the picture and the barbarous lessons he had learnt in the trenches.

It is in dialogue with pain that many beautiful things acquire their value. Acquaintance with grief turns out to be one of the more unusual prerequisites of architectural appreciation. We might, quite aside from all other requirements, need to be a little sad before buildings can properly touch us.

9.

Taking architecture seriously therefore makes some singular and strenuous demands upon us. It requires that we open ourselves to the idea that we are affected by our surroundings even when they are made of vinyl and would be expensive and time-consuming to ameliorate. It means conceding that we are inconveniently vulnerable to the colour of our wallpaper and that our sense of purpose may be derailed by an unfortunate bedspread. At the same time, it means acknowledging that buildings are able to solve no more than a fraction of our dissatisfactions or prevent evil from unfolding under their watch. Architecture, even at its most accomplished, will only ever constitute a small, and imperfect (expensive, prone to destruction and morally unreliable), protest against the state of things. More awkwardly still, architecture asks us to imagine that happiness might often have an unostentatious, unheroic character to it, that it might be found in a run of old floorboards or in a wash of morning light over a plaster wall – in undramatic, frangible scenes of beauty that move us because we are aware of the darker backdrop against which they are set.

10.

But if we accept the legitimacy of the subject nevertheless, then a new and contentious series of questions at once opens up. We have to confront the vexed point on which so much of the history of architecture pivots. We have to ask what exactly a beautiful building might look like.

Ludwig Wittgenstein, having abandoned academia for three years in order to construct a house for his sister Gretl in Vienna, understood the magnitude of the challenge. 'You think philosophy is difficult,' observed the author of the *Tractatus Logico-Philosophicus*, 'but I tell you, it is nothing compared to the difficulty of being a good architect.'

II. In What Style Shall We Build?

1.

What is a beautiful building? To be modern is to experience this as an awkward and possibly unanswerable question, the very notion of beauty having come to seem like a concept doomed to ignite unfruitful and childish argument. How can anyone claim to know what is attractive? How can anyone adjudicate between the competing claims of different styles or defend a particular choice in the face of the contradictory tastes of others? The creation of beauty, once viewed as the central task of the architect, has quietly evaporated from serious professional discussion and retreated to a confused private imperative.

2.

It wasn't always thought so hard to know how to build beautifully. For over a thousand discontinuous years in the history of the West, a beautiful building was synonymous with a Classical building, a structure with a temple front, decorated columns, repeated ratios and a symmetrical façade.

The Greeks gave birth to the Classical style, the Romans copied and developed it, and, after a gap of a thousand years, the educated classes of Renaissance Italy rediscovered it. From the peninsula, Classicism spread north and west, it took on local accents and was articulated in new materials. Classical buildings appeared as far apart as Helsinki and Budapest, Savannah and St Petersburg. The sensibility was applied to interiors, to Classical chairs and ceilings, beds and baths.

Alhough it is the differences between varieties of Classicism that have tended to interest historians most, it is the similarities that are ultimately more striking. For hundreds of years there was near unanimity about how to construct a window or a door, how to fashion columns and pedimented fronts, how to relate rooms to hallways and how to model ironwork and mouldings – assumptions codified by Renaissance scholar–architects and popularised in pattern books for ordinary builders.

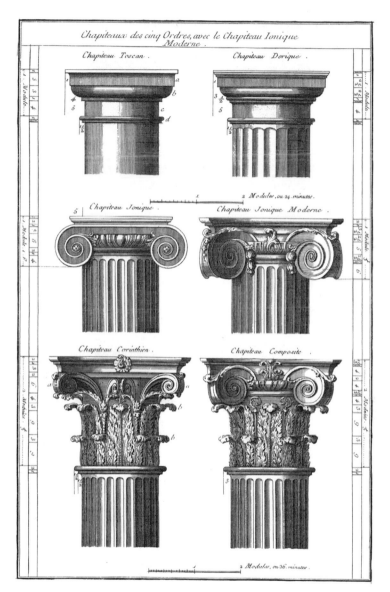

Rules for Classical columns:
Architectural plate from Denis Diderot, editor, *Encyclopédie*, 1780

A city-wide consensus about beauty:
John Wood the Elder, north side, Queen Square, Bath, 1736

Left: The Arch of Constantine, Rome, *c.* AD 315
Right: Robert Adam, rear elevation, Kedleston Hall, 1765

So strong was this consensus that whole cities achieved a stylistic unity that stretched across successions of squares and avenues. An aesthetic language dating back to the Temple of Apollo at Delphi ended up gracing the family homes of Edinburgh accountants and Philadelphia lawyers.

Few Classical architects or their clients felt any impulse towards originality. Fidelity to the canon was what mattered; repetition was the norm. When Robert Adam designed Kedleston Hall (1765), it was a point of pride for him to embed an exact reproduction of the Arch of Constantine (*c.* 315) in the middle of the rear elevation. Thomas Hamilton's High School in Edinburgh (1825), though it was made of sombre grey Craigleith sandstone, sat under sepulchral Scottish skies and had steel beams supporting its roof, was lauded for the skill with which it imitated the form of the Doric Temple of the Parthenon in Athens (*c.* 438 BC). Thomas Jefferson's campus for the University of Virginia, in Charlottesville (1826), quoted without shame from the Roman Temple of Fortuna Virilis (*c.* 100 BC) and the Baths of Diocletian (AD 302), while Joseph Hansom's new town hall in Birmingham (1832) was a faithful adaptation, set down in the middle of an industrial city, of the Roman Maison Carrée at Nîmes (*c.* AD 130).

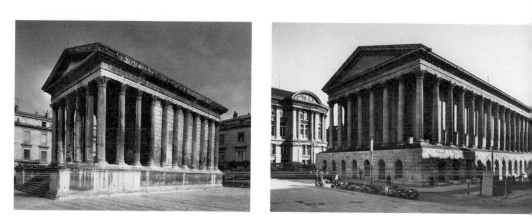

Left: Maison Carrée, Nîmes, c. AD 130
Right: Joseph Hansom, Town Hall, Birmingham, 1832

Thus large parts of the man-made world in the early-modern period would not, in their outward appearance at least, have shaken many of the architectural assumptions of a magically resurrected contemporary of the Roman emperor Marcus Aurelius.

3.

When it came to simpler, cheaper houses, there was again a consensus about the most fitting way to build, though here the canon was the result not of any common cultural vision but of a host of limitations.

Foremost among these was climate, which, in the absence of affordable technology to resist it, usually dictated an austere menu of options for how most sensibly to put up a wall, pitch a roof or render a façade. The expense of transporting materials over any significant distance likewise limited stylistic choice, forcing the majority of householders to settle uncomplainingly for available stone, wood or mud. The difficulties of travel also hindered the spread of knowledge about alternative building methods. Printing costs meant that few ever saw so much as a picture of how houses looked in other parts of the world (which explains why, in so much of early northern religious art, Jesus is born in what appears to be a chalet).

Limitations bred strong local architectural identities. Within a certain radius, houses would uniformly be constructed of a particular native material, which would cede its ubiquity to another on the opposite side of a river or a mountain range. An ordinary Kentish house could thus be distinguished at a glance from a Cornish one, or a farm in the Jura from one in the Engadine. In most areas, houses continued to be built as they had always been built, using whatever was around, with an absence of aesthetic self-consciousness, with their owners' modest pride at being able to afford shelter in the first place.

4.

Then, in the spring of 1747, an effeminate young man with a taste for luxury, lace collars and gossip bought a former coachman's cottage on forty acres of land in Twickenham on the River Thames – and set about building himself a villa which gravely complicated the prevailing sense of what a beautiful house might look like.

Any number of architects could have furnished Horace Walpole, the youngest son of the British prime minister, Sir Robert, with something conventional for his new estate, a Palladian mansion, perhaps a little like his father's home, Houghton Hall, on the north Norfolk coast. But in architecture, as in dress, conversation and choice of career, Walpole prided himself on being different. In spite of his Classical education, his real interest lay in the medieval period, which thrilled him with its iconography of ruined abbeys, moonlit nights, graveyards and (especially) crusaders in armour. Walpole therefore decided to build himself the world's first Gothic house.

Because no one before him had ever attempted to apply the ecclesiastical idiom of the Middle Ages to a domestic setting, Walpole had to be resourceful. He modelled his fireplace on the tomb of Archbishop

Few ever saw so much as a picture of how houses looked in other parts of the world:
Smallhythe Place, Tenterden, Kent, early sixteenth century

A new understanding of domestic beauty:
Horace Walpole, Strawberry Hill, Twickenham, 1750–92

Bouchier in Canterbury Cathedral, copied the design of his library shelves from the tomb of Aymer de Valence in Westminster Abbey, and derived the ceiling of his main hall from the quatrefoil compartments and rosettes of the Abbey's Chapel of Henry VII.

When he was done, being temperamentally disinclined to keep any of his achievements quiet, Walpole invited for a tour everyone he knew,

The Long Gallery, Strawberry Hill

which included most of the opinion-formers and gentry of the land. For good measure, he issued tickets to the general public as well.

After a viewing, many of Walpole's astonished guests began to wonder if they, too, might not dare to abandon the Classical mode in favour of the Gothic. The fashion started modestly enough, with the construction of the occasional seaside or suburban villa, but, within a few decades, a

The most noble and appropriate architecture of all:
Imre Steindl, Houses of Parliament, Budapest, 1904

revolution in taste was under way which would shake to the core the assumptions on which the Classical consensus had formerly rested. Gothic buildings began to appear in Britain, then across Europe and North America. Transcending its origins as the fancy of a dilettante, the style acquired architectural seriousness and prestige, to the extent that, just fifty or so years after Walpole broke ground at Strawberry Hill, defenders of Gothic could claim – much in the way that the Classicists had done before them – that theirs was the most noble and appropriate architecture of all, the natural choice for both domestic buildings and the parliaments and universities of the great nations.

5.

The factors which fostered the Gothic revival – greater historical awareness, improved transport links, a new clientele impatient for variety – soon enough generated curiosity about the architectural styles of other eras and lands. By the early nineteenth century, in most Western countries, anyone contemplating putting up a house was faced with an unprecedented array of choices regarding its appearance.

Architects boasted of their ability to turn out houses in Indian, Chinese, Egyptian, Islamic, Tyrolean or Jacobean styles, or in any combination of these. Among the most versatile of the new polymaths was an Englishman named Humphry Repton, who earned a reputation for presenting hesitant clients with detailed drawings of the many stylistic options available to them.

For those of more modest means, new pattern books were created, the most popular of which, John Loudon's *The Encyclopaedia of Cottage, Farm and Villa Architecture* (1833), presented self-builders with plans enabling them to construct houses from any part of the world, an initiative which rapidly wiped out regional types of architecture.

GRECIAN

GOTHIC

Options for your next home:
Humphry Repton, *Characters of Houses*, 1816

Left to right: Swiss style cottage and Old English style cottage
From John Loudon, *The Encyclopaedia of Cottage, Farm and Villa Architecture*, 1833

Changes in the way property was developed served to promote further opportunities for eclecticism. In the eighteenth century, London, like most cities in Europe, had expanded primarily through the efforts of aristocratic landowners, who gave their names to the squares which they carved across their old farms and fields: Lord Southampton, the Earl of Bedford, Sir Richard Grosvenor and the Duke of Portland. These were men of shared taste: comfortable in Latin and Greek, students of Cicero and Tacitus, and unambivalent proponents of the Classical style. When the Earl of Bedford issued contracts for the building of his eponymous square in 1776, his stipulations revealed an almost maniacal obsession with Classical harmony, setting down as they did rules to govern the exact height of each storey, the depth of every window frame, the colour of the bricks and the specific kind of wood to be used in the floorboards ('the best Memel or Riga timber without a trace of sap'). So concerned was the earl with Classical proportion and precision that he regularly rose at dawn and went out with a pair of garden scissors to ensure that the bushes at the centre of his square were trained to grow symmetrically.

But in the century that followed, royals and aristocrats withdrew from speculative construction even as demand for housing exploded. Those

A vanishing Classical consensus about beauty:
Bedford Square, London, 1783

New visions of beauty:
John Foulston, Kerr Street, Devonport, Plymouth, 1824

Front elevation, Castle Ward, Strangford Lough, 1767

who came in their wake were not typically readers of Cicero and Tacitus. More often, they were entrepreneurs with a penchant for variety and whimsy. Instinctively scornful of the martial sobriety of the Classical tradition, they competed to attract clients through the playfulness and exuberance of their developments, as epitomised by a street in Plymouth which combined, within only a few hundred metres, a row of Roman Corinthian terraced houses, a Doric town hall, an Oriental chapel, a pair of private homes in the Ionic style and an Egyptian library.

6.

The only problem with unrestricted choice, however, is that it tends not to lie so far from outright chaos.

The danger inherent in such freedom first and famously broke through on the shores of a quiet lough in Northern Ireland, where, around the

Rear elevation, Castle Ward

middle of the eighteenth century, a local aristocrat and his wife decided to build themselves a house. Both passionate about architecture, Viscount Bangor and Lady Anne Bligh nevertheless found that they couldn't agree on an appropriate style. The viscount was a Classicist. He wanted something with three bays, engaged columns, Palladian proportions and windows topped with triangular consoled pediments. Anne, in contrast, was keener on the Gothic, preferring castellated roofs with pinnacles, centre-pointed windows and quatrefoils. She had heard about the ceilings at Strawberry Hill and longed to have a few of her own. The struggle grew stubborn and ill-natured, until the couple's architect came up with a solution of Solomonic ingenuity: he would divide the house in two. The front half was built in the Classical style, the rear in the Gothic. The compromise continued inside, with the music room and stairwell being Classical in feeling, embellished with Doric friezes and columns, while the boudoir and private rooms had a Gothic air, complete with fan-vaulted ceilings and pointed-arched fireplaces.

The more sensitive critics were appalled and, with such buildings in mind, began an ardent search for a way to restore a measure of visual consensus. 'We suffer from a *carnival* of architecture,' complained Augustus Pugin in 1836. 'Private judgement runs riot. Every architect has a theory of his own.' In 1828 a young German practitioner named Heinrich Hübsch published a book whose title characterised the dilemma of an entire age: *In What Style Shall We Build?* There had to be a way for the defenders of the Gothic, Old English and Swiss styles to resolve their disputes; there had to be a way of knowing whether to furnish the dining room with Ancient Egyptian or Chinese chairs; a way of giving the upper hand to either Lady Anne or Viscount Bangor – and thus of ensuring that houses would never again be built facing in two different directions.

But where could such a principle be found? Just what style were architects to build in?

7.

The answer that eventually emerged was not really an answer; rather, it was an admonishment that it might be irrelevant and even indulgent to raise the question in the first place.

A prohibition against discussions of beauty in architecture was imposed by a new breed of men, engineers, who had achieved professional recognition only in the late eighteenth century, but had thereafter risen quickly to dominance in the construction of the new buildings of the Industrial Revolution. Mastering the technologies of iron and steel, of plate glass and concrete, they drew interest and inspired awe with their bridges, railway hangars, aqueducts and docks. More novel even than their abilities, perhaps, was the fact that they seemed to complete these projects without ever directly asking themselves what style it was best to adopt.

Charged with erecting a bridge, they tried to design the lightest possible frame that could stretch over the widest span at the lowest cost. When they built a railway station, they aimed for a hall that would allow steam to disperse safely, let in a large amount of natural light and accommodate a constant crowd of travellers. They demanded that factories be able to house unwieldy machinery and that steamships carry cargoes of impatient passengers punctually across heavy seas. But they did not appear to give much thought to whether there should be a Corinthian or a Doric set of capitals gracing the upper galleries of a ship, whether a Chinese dragon might look pleasing at the end of a locomotive or whether suburban gas works should be done up in a Tuscan or Islamic style.

Yet, despite this indifference, the new men of science seemed capable of building the most impressive and, in many cases, the most seductive structures of their confused age.

8.

The philosophy of the engineers flew in the face of everything the architectural profession had ever stood for. 'To turn something useful, practical, functional into something beautiful, that is architecture's duty,' insisted Karl Friedrich Schinkel. 'Architecture, as distinguished from mere building, is the decoration of construction,' echoed Sir George Gilbert Scott. If the Doge's Palace deserved to be classified as great architecture, it was not because the roof was watertight or because it provided Venice's civil servants with the necessary number of meeting rooms but rather, the architects defensively suggested, because it sported carvings on its roof, a delicate arrangement of white and pink bricks on its façades, and deliberately slender, tapering, pointed arches throughout – details that would have had no place in a design by a graduate of the École Polytechnique in Paris or the Engineering Academy of Dresden. The essence of great architecture was understood to reside in what was functionally unnecessary.

The irrelevance of aesthetic discussion:
John Fowler, Benjamin Baker, Forth Railway Bridge,
construction of the central girder, September 1889

'To turn something useful, practical, functional into something beautiful, that is architecture's duty':
Doge's Palace (detail), Venice, 1340–1420

9.

The principles of engineering may have brutally contradicted those of architecture, but a vocal minority of nineteenth-century architects nevertheless perceived that the engineers were capable of providing them with a critical key to their salvation – for what these men had, and they so sorely lacked, was certainty. The engineers had landed on an apparently impregnable method of evaluating the wisdom of a design: they felt confidently able to declare that a structure was correct and honest in so far as it performed its mechanical functions efficiently; and false and immoral in so far as it was burdened with non-supporting pillars, decorative statues, frescos or carvings.

Exchanging discussions of beauty for considerations of function promised to move architecture away from a morass of perplexing, insoluble disputes about aesthetics towards an uncontentious pursuit of technological truth, ensuring that it might henceforth be as peculiar to argue about the appearance of a building as it would be to argue about the answer to a simple algebraic equation.

With functional principles standing as a new measure of worth, the entire history of architecture could be scanned and its masterworks reassessed in terms of their relative degrees of veracity and falsehood. The Romans were deemed dishonest for having added columns to the Colosseum, because these elegantly sculpted, costly pieces of stone only *pretended* to support the upper storeys, whereas in fact – as any engineer could see – the whole structure was being held up by the arches alone.

Equally, Johann Balthasar Neumann had lied in almost every aspect of his Vierzehnheiligen Pilgrimage Church in Banz. Here the inside walls made a show of holding up the building, but in reality that task fell to a separate and hidden frame. Even Neumann's domed, painted ceiling had nothing to do with the real roof but was merely a stucco skin nestled beneath the actual, conventionally pitched design.

A mendacious ceiling:
Johann Balthasar Neumann, Vierzehnheiligen Pilgrimage Church, Banz, 1772

Charles Cockerell, Ashmolean and Taylorian Institute, Oxford, 1840

Similarly, Charles Cockerell was judged to have been almost disgracefully deceptive and wasteful in his design for the Ashmolean Museum and Taylorian Institute in Oxford. His crime had been to place massive Ionic columns, which could have supported four storeys' worth of masonry, around the outside of the building, where they carried nothing heavier than pots and statues, while leaving the real weight of the structure to be borne by another set of columns concealed within the walls.

10.

But what would a house look like whose architect had renounced any interest in beauty in order to focus exclusively on mechanical functioning? To believe its creator in certain of his moods, it might resemble the Villa Savoye.

In the spring of 1928 a Parisian couple named Pierre and Emilie Savoye approached the 41-year-old Swiss architect Le Corbusier and asked him to design a country house for them and their young son Roger on a wooded plot of land they owned overlooking the Seine, in Poissy, west of Paris. Le Corbusier had by this point in his career built fifteen private houses and acquired international renown for his categorical views on architecture.

'Our engineers are healthy and virile, active and useful, balanced and happy in their work,' he exclaimed in *Towards a New Architecture* (1923), while 'our architects are disillusioned and unemployed, boastful or peevish. This is because there will soon be nothing more for them to do. We no longer have the money to erect historical souvenirs. At the same time, everyone needs to wash! Our engineers provide for these things and so they will be our builders.'

Le Corbusier recommended that the houses of the future be ascetic and clean, disciplined and frugal. His hatred of any kind of decoration extended to a pity for the British Royal Family and the ornate, golden

THE ROME OF HORRORS

From Le Corbusier, *Towards a New Architecture*, 1923

carriage in which they travelled to open Parliament every year. He suggested that they push the carved monstrosity off the cliffs of Dover and instead learn to travel around their realm in a Hispano-Suiza 1911 racing car. He even mocked Rome, the traditional destination for the education and edification of young architects, and renamed it the 'city of horrors', 'the damnation of the half-educated' and 'the cancer of French architecture' – on account of its violation of functional principles through an abundance of Baroque detailing, wall-painting and statuary.

For Le Corbusier, true, great architecture – meaning, architecture motivated by the quest for efficiency – was more likely to be found in a 40,000-kilowatt electricity turbine or a low-pressure ventilating fan. It was to these machines that his books accorded the reverential photographs which previous architectural writers had reserved for cathedrals and opera houses.

Once asked by a magazine editor to name his favourite chair, Le Corbusier cited the seat of a cockpit, and described the first time he ever saw an aeroplane, in the spring of 1909, in the sky above Paris – it was the aviator the Comte de Lambert taking a turn around the Eiffel Tower

Things like this were being built at the same time as our railroads.

From Le Corbusier, *The City of Tomorrow and Its Planning*, 1925

A LOW-PRESSURE VENTILATING FAN   40,000 KILOWATT TURBINE FOR ELECTRICITY

From Le Corbusier, *Towards a New Architecture*, 1923

– as the most significant moment of his life. He observed that the requirements of flight of necessity rid aeroplanes of all superfluous decoration and so unwittingly transformed them into successful pieces of architecture. To place a Classical statue atop a house was as absurd as to add one to a plane, he noted, but at least by crashing in response to this addition, the plane had the advantage of rendering its absurdity starkly manifest. 'L'avion accuse,' he concluded.

But if the function of a plane was to fly, what was the function of a house? Le Corbusier arrived ('scientifically' he assured his readers) at a simple list of requirements, beyond which all other ambitions were no more than 'romantic cobwebs'. The function of a house was, he wrote, to provide: '1. A shelter against heat, cold, rain, thieves and the inquisitive. 2. A receptacle for light and sun. 3. A certain number of cells appropriated to cooking, work, and personal life.'

11.

Behind a wall on the summit of a hill in Poissy, a gravel path curves through dense trees before opening out into a clearing, in the middle of which stands a thin, white, rectangular box, with ribbon windows running along its sides, supported off the ground on a series of implausibly slender pillars. A structure on the roof of the Villa Savoye resembles a water tower or gas cylinder, but turns out on closer inspection to be a terrace with a semicircular protecting wall. The house looks like a piece of finely tooled precision machinery, some industrial object of unknown purpose, with flawless white surfaces that on a bright day reflect back the sun with the luminescent intensity of fishermen's cottages on the islands of the Aegean. It seems that the house may be no more than a temporary visitor and that its roof-top equipment could at any point receive a signal that would lead it to fire its concealed engines and rise slowly over the surrounding trees and historically styled villas on the beginning of a long journey home to a remote galaxy.

The influence of science and aeronautics continues inside. A front door made of steel opens onto a hallway as clean, bright and bare as an operating theatre. There are tiles on the floor, naked bulbs on the ceiling and, in the middle of the hall, a basin which invites guests to cleanse themselves of the impurities of the outside world. Dominating the room is a large ramp with a simple tubular rail which leads up to the main living quarters. Here a large kitchen is equipped with all the conveniences of its era. Steel-framed strip windows feed natural light into the principal rooms. The bathrooms are shrines to hygiene and athleticism; the exposed pipe work would do justice to a submarine.

Even in these intimate spaces, the mood remains technical and astringent. There is nothing extraneous or decorative here, no rosettes or mouldings, no flourishes or ornaments. Walls meet ceilings at perfect right angles, without the softening influence of borders. The visual language is drawn exclusively from industry, the artificial light provided by factory lamps. There are few pieces of furniture, for Le Corbusier had recommended to his clients that they keep their belongings to a minimum, reacting with injured alarm when Madame Savoye expressed a desire

Le Corbusier, living room, Villa Savoye, Poissy, 1931

to fit an armchair and two sofas in the living room. 'Home life today is being paralysed by the deplorable notion that we must have furniture,' her architect protested. 'This notion should be rooted out and replaced by that of *equipment*.'

'What [modern man] wants is a monk's cell, well lit and heated, with a corner from which he can look at the stars,' Le Corbusier had written. As the builders finished their work, the Savoye family had reason to feel confident that in the house he had designed for them, these aspirations, at least, would be consummately met.

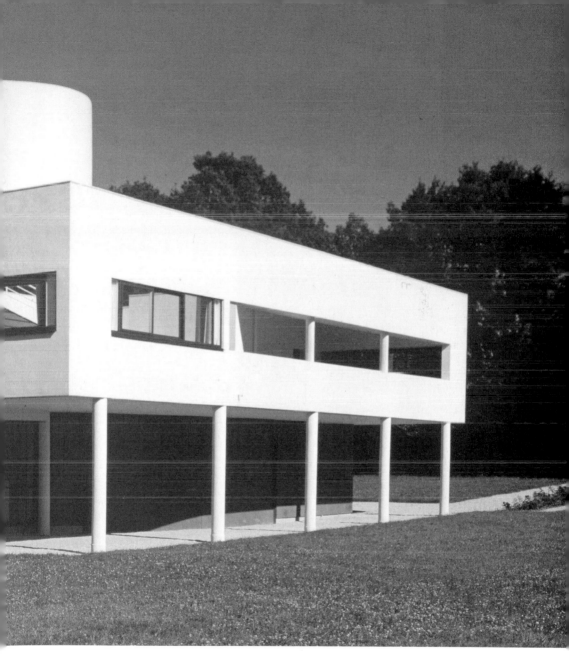

Le Corbusier, Villa Savoye, Poissy, 1931

12.

Governed by an ethos conceived by engineers, Modernism claimed to have supplied a definitive answer to the question of beauty in architecture: the point of a house was not to be beautiful but to function well.

Yet this neat separation between the vexed matter of appearance and the more straightforward one of performance has always hung on an illusory distinction. Although we may at first glance associate the word 'function' with the efficient provision of physical sanctuary, we are in the end unlikely to respect a structure which does no more than keep us dry and warm.

Of almost any building, we ask not only that it do a certain thing but also that it look a certain way, that it contribute to a given mood: of religiosity or scholarship, rusticity or modernity, commerce or domesticity. We may require it to generate a feeling of reassurance or of excitement, of harmony or of containment. We may hope that it will connect us to the past or stand as a symbol of the future, and we would complain, no less than we would about a malfunctioning bathroom, if this second, aesthetic, expressive level of function were left unattended.

In a more encompassing suggestion, John Ruskin proposed that we seek two things of our buildings. We want them to shelter us. And we want them to *speak* to us – to speak to us of whatever we find important and need to be reminded of.

13.

In reality, the architects of the Modernist movement, just like all their predecessors, wanted their houses to speak. Only not of the nineteenth century. Or of privilege and aristocratic life. Or of the Middle Ages or Ancient Rome. They wanted their houses to speak of the future, with its promise of speed and technology, democracy and science. They wanted their armchairs to evoke racing cars and planes, they wanted their lamps to evoke the power of industry and their coffee pots the dynamism of high-speed trains.

It wasn't that they ever lost sight of the importance of arousing feelings; their argument was, instead, with the family of feelings that previous architectural styles had generated.

With his central staircase in the Villa Savoye, Le Corbusier – just like Ange-Jacques Gabriel at the Classical pavilion of Le Petit Trianon in Versailles, a few miles to the south – was trying to do something other than simply carry people to an upper floor. He was trying to prompt a state of the soul.

Despite their claims to a purely scientific and reasoned approach, the relationship of Modernist architects to their work remained at base a romantic one: they looked to architecture to support a way of life that appealed to them. Their domestic buildings were conceived as stage sets for actors in an idealised drama about contemporary existence.

Two staircases to prompt two different states of the soul:
Left: Le Petit Trianon, Versailles, 1768
Right: Villa Savoye, Poissy, 1931

A stage set for actors in an idealised drama about contemporary existence:
Advertisement for the 1927 Mercedes-Benz, set against Le Corbusier and Pierre
Jeanneret's Double-house, Weissenhofsiedlung, Stuttgart, 1927

14.

So strong was the aesthetic interest of the Modernists that it routinely took precedence over considerations of efficiency. The Villa Savoye might have looked like a practically minded machine, but it was in reality an artistically motivated folly. The bare walls were handmade by artisans using costly imported Swiss mortar, they were as delicate as pieces of lace and as devoted to generating feelings as the jewel-encrusted naves of a Counter-Reformation Church.

By Modernism's own standards, the roof of the villa was equally, and yet more ruinously, dishonest. In spite of initial protests from the Savoyes, Le Corbusier insisted – supposedly on technical and economic grounds alone – that a flat roof would be preferable to a pitched one. It would, he assured his clients, be cheaper to construct, easier to maintain and cooler in summer, and Madame Savoye would be able to do her gymnastic exercises on it without being bothered by damp vapours emanating from the ground floor. But only a week after the family moved in, the roof sprang a leak over Roger's bedroom, letting in so much water that the boy contracted a chest infection, which turned into pneumonia, which eventually required him to spend a year recuperating in a sanatorium in Chamonix. In September 1936, six years after the villa's official completion, Madame Savoye compressed her feelings about the performance of the flat roof into a (rain-splattered) letter: 'It's raining in the hall, it's raining on the ramp, and the wall of the garage is absolutely soaked. What's more, it's still raining in my bathroom, which floods in bad weather, as the water comes in through the skylight.' Le Corbusier promised that the problem would be fixed straightaway, then took the opportunity to remind his client of how enthusiastically his flat-roofed design had been received by architectural critics worldwide: 'You should place a book on the table in the downstairs hall and ask all your visitors to inscribe their names and addresses in it. You'll see how many fine autographs you will collect'. But this invitation

Beautiful but not rain-proof:
Rooftop, Villa Savoye, 1931

to philography was of little comfort to the rheumatic Savoye family. 'After innumerable demands on my part, you have finally accepted that this house which you built in 1929 is uninhabitable,' admonished Madame Savoye in the autumn of 1937. 'Your responsibility is at stake and I have no need to foot the bill. Please render it habitable immediately. I sincerely hope that I will not have to take recourse to legal action.' Only the outbreak of the Second World War and the Savoye family's consequent flight from Paris saved Le Corbusier from having to answer in a courtroom for the design of his largely uninhabitable, if extraordinarily beautiful, machine-for-living.

15.

If Modernist architects privately designed with beauty in mind, why did they justify their work principally in technological terms?

Fear seems to have lain at the heart of their discretion. The end of a belief in a universal standard of beauty had created a climate in which no one style could be immune from criticism. Objections to the appearance of Modernist houses, voiced by adherents of Gothic or Tyrolean architecture, could not be shrugged off without inviting accusations of high-handedness and arrogance. In aesthetics, as in democratic politics, a final arbiter had grown elusive.

Hence the attractions of a scientific language with which to ward off detractors and convince the wavering. Even the God of the Old Testament, faced with the continual querulousness of the tribes of Israel, had occasionally to ignite a piece of desert shrub to awe his audience into reverence. Technology would be the Modernists' burning bush. To speak of technology in relation to one's houses was to appeal – now that the influence of Christianity was waning and Classical culture was being ignored – to the most prestigious force in society, responsible for penicillin, telephones and aeroplanes. Science, then, would apparently determine the pitch of the roof.

16.

Yet, in truth, science is rarely so categorical. In 1925 the architect and designer Marcel Breuer unveiled a chair which he touted as the world's first soberly logical solution to 'the problem of sitting'. Every part of the B3 chair was the result, he explained, of an intensive effort to banish 'the whimsical in favour of the rational'.

The B3's seat and back were made of leather for durability; its offset angular shape was the inevitable answer to the needs of the human vertebrae; and its steel frame, because it was a hundred times stronger than wood, would never splinter or chip.

But Breuer's attempt to make a scientific case for his chair could not breach an impregnable reality: while it may be necessary to resort to specific materials and forms when constructing a bridge, there is no corresponding technical need to limit one's imagination in designing a piece of living-room furniture, which must merely support the weight of a human body – and so can be built of curved steel but also as happily of oak, bamboo, plastic or fibreglass. A chair can equally well satisfy its modest brief in the guise of a B3, a Queen Anne or a Windsor armchair. Science alone cannot tell us how our seats should look.

Even in more complex commissions, the laws of engineering seldom dictate a particular style. The Montjuïc Telecommunications Tower in Barcelona, for example, could have taken on any number of forms while still managing to transmit its signals adequately. The antenna could have been sculpted to look like a pear rather than like a javelin; the base might have been made to resemble a riding boot rather than the prow of a spacecraft. Dozens of options would have each worked well mechanically. But as its architect, Santiago Calatrava, recognised, only a very few designs would have conveyed with appropriate poetry the promises of modernity to the people of Barcelona.

17.

The incoherencies of the Modernist relationship to science return us to the confusing plethora of architectural options that the early Modernists had once hoped to eradicate. We return to the carnival of architecture. Why not carve flowers on our buildings? Why not use concrete panels imprinted with pictures of aeroplanes and insects? Why not coat a skyscraper with Islamic motifs?

If engineering cannot tell us what our houses should look like, nor in a pluralistic and non-deferential world can precedent or tradition, we must be free to pursue all stylistic options. We should acknowledge that the

A chair dictated by science?
Marcel Breuer, B3 chair, 1925

Functional chairs:
Left: Queen Anne japanned armchair, *c.* 1710
Right: High-back Windsor armchair, 1850s

question of what is beautiful is both impossible to elucidate and shameful and even undemocratic to mention.

18.
However, there might be a way to surmount this state of sterile relativism with the help of John Ruskin's provocative remark about the eloquence of architecture. The remark focuses our minds on the idea that buildings are not simply visual objects without any connection to concepts which we can analyse and then evaluate. Buildings *speak* – and on topics which can readily be discerned. They speak of democracy or aristocracy, openness or arrogance, welcome or threat, a sympathy for the future or a hankering for the past.

Art rather than science:
Opposite: Santiago Calatrava, Montjuïc Telecommunications Tower, Barcelona, 1991
The return of choice:
Left: Herzog & de Meuron, Library of the Eberswalde Technical School, Eberswalde, 1999
Right: Jean Nouvel, proposed skyscraper, Doha, 2004

Left: Tias Eckhoff, Regent Service, Porsgrund, 1961
Right: Blue Cameo Service, Sèvres, 1778

Any object of design will give off an impression of the psychological and moral attitudes it supports. We can, for example, feel two distinct conceptions of fulfilment emanating from a plain Scandinavian crockery set on the one hand and an ornate Sèvres one on the other – an invitation to a democratic graceful sensibility in the former case, to a ceremonial and class-bound disposition in the latter.

In essence, what works of design and architecture talk to us about is the kind of life that would most appropriately unfold within and around them. They tell us of certain moods that they seek to encourage and sustain in their inhabitants. While keeping us warm and helping us in mechanical ways, they simultaneously hold out an invitation for us to be specific sorts of people. They speak of visions of happiness.

To describe a building as beautiful therefore suggests more than a mere aesthetic fondness; it implies an attraction to the particular way of life this structure is promoting through its roof, door handles, window frames, staircase and furnishings. A feeling of beauty is a sign that we have come upon a material articulation of certain of our ideas of a good life.

Similarly, buildings will strike us as offensive not because they violate a private and mysterious visual preference but because they conflict with our understanding of the rightful sense of existence – which helps to explain the seriousness and viciousness with which disputes about fitting architecture tend to unfold.

19.

The advantage of shifting the focus of discussion away from the strictly visual towards the values promoted by buildings is that we become able to handle talk about the appearance of works of architecture rather as we do wider debates about people, ideas and political agendas.

Arguments about what is beautiful emerge as no easier to resolve, but then again no harder, than disputes about what is wise or right. We can learn to defend or attack a concept of beauty in the same way we might defend or attack a legal position or an ethical stance. We can understand, and publically explain, why we believe a building to be desirable or offensive on the basis of the things it talks to us about.

The notion of buildings that speak helps us to place at the very centre of our architectural conundrums the question of the values we want to live by – rather than merely of how we want things to look.

What do we want our buildings to talk to us about?
Left: Michael Shanly Homes, Oakington Place, Middlesex, 2005
Right: Office of Makoto Yamaguchi, Villa, Karuizawa, 2003

III. Talking Buildings

1.

If our interest in buildings and objects is indeed determined as much by what they say to us as by how they perform their material functions, it is worth elaborating on the curious process by which arrangements of stone, steel, concrete, wood and glass seem able to express themselves – and can on rare occasions leave us under the impression that they are talking to us about significant and touching things.

2.

We will, of course, run a risk if we spend extended periods analysing the meanings that emanate from practical objects. To be preoccupied with deciphering the message encoded in a light switch or a tap is to leave ourselves more than usually vulnerable to the commonsensical scorn of those who seek little from such fittings beyond a means of illuminating their bedroom or rinsing their teeth.

To inoculate ourselves against this derision, and to gain confidence in cultivating a contrary, more meditative attitude towards objects, we might profitably pay a visit to a museum of modern art. In whitewashed galleries housing collections of twentieth-century abstract sculpture, we are offered a rare perspective on how exactly three-dimensional masses can assume and convey meaning – a perspective that may in turn enable us to regard our fittings and houses in a new way.

3.

It was in the first half of the twentieth century that sculptors began eliciting equal measures of awe and opprobrium for exhibiting pieces to which it seemed hard to put a name, works that both lacked an interest in the mimetic ambitions that had dominated Western sculpture since the Ancient Greeks and, despite a certain resemblance to domestic furnishings, had no practical capacities either.

What abstract objects can say:
Henry Moore, *Two Forms*, 1934

Yet, notwithstanding these limitations, abstract artists argued that their sculptures were capable of articulating the greatest of themes. Many critics agreed. Herbert Read described Henry Moore's work as a treatise on human kindness and cruelty in a world from which God had recently departed, while for David Sylvester, Alberto Giacometti's sculptures expressed the loneliness and desire of man alienated from his authentic self in industrial society.

It may be easy to laugh at the grandiloquence of claims directed at objects which on occasion resemble giant earplugs or upturned lawn-mowers. But, instead of accusing critics of reading too much into too little, we should allow abstract sculptures to demonstrate to us the range of thoughts and emotions that every kind of non-representational object can convey. The gift of the most talented sculptors has been to teach us that large ideas, for example, about intelligence or kindness, youth or seren-ity, can be communicated in chunks of wood and string, or in plaster and metal contraptions, as well as they can in words or in human or animal likenesses. The great abstract sculptures have succeeded in speaking to us, in their peculiar dissociated language, of the important themes of our lives.

In turn, these sculptures afford us an opportunity to focus with unac-customed intensity on the communicative powers of all objects, including our buildings and their furnishings. Inspired by a museum visit, we may scold ourselves for our previous prosaic belief that a salad bowl is only a salad bowl, rather than, in truth, an object over which there linger faint but meaningful associations of wholeness, the feminine and the infinite. We can look at a practical entity like a desk, a column or an entire apart-ment building and here, too, locate abstract articulations of some of the important themes of our lives.

Top: Alberto Giacometti, *Hour of the Traces*, 1930; Jasper Morrison, ATM Table, 2003
Middle: Anthony Caro, *Whispering*, 1969; Mies van der Rohe, column, Barcelona Pavilion, 1929
Bottom: Donald Judd, *Untitled*, 1989; Diener and Diener, Migros, Lucerne, 2000

4.

A bright morning in the Tate Gallery, St Ives, Cornwall. On a plinth sits a marble sculpture by Barbara Hepworth, first exhibited in 1936. Although it is unclear what exactly these three stones might mean or represent – a mystery reflected in their reticent title, *Two Segments and a Sphere* – they nevertheless manage to arrest and reward our gaze. Their interest centres on the opposition between the ball and the semicircular wedge on which it rests. The ball looks unstable and energetic; we sense how keenly it wants to roll down the segment's leading edge and bowl across the room. By contrast with this impulsiveness, the accompanying wedge conveys maturity and stability: it seems content to nurse gently from side to side, taming the recklessness of its charge. In viewing the piece, we are witness to a tender and playful relationship, rendered majestic through the primordial medium of polished white marble.

In an essay on Hepworth, the psychoanalytic critic Adrian Stokes attempted to analyse the power of this apparently simple work. He arrived at a compelling conclusion. If the sculpture touches us, he ventured, it may be because we unconsciously understand it as a family portrait. The mobility and chubby fullness of the sphere subtly suggest to us a wriggling fat-cheeked baby, while the rocking ample forms of the segment have echoes of a calm, indulgent, broad-hipped mother. We dimly apprehend in the whole a central theme of our lives. We sense a parable in stone about motherly love.

Stokes's argument directs us to two ideas. First, that it doesn't take much for us to interpret an object as a human or animal figure. A piece of stone can have no legs, eyes, ears or almost any of the features associated with a living thing; it need have only the merest hint of a maternal thigh or a babyish cheek and we will start to read it as a character. Thanks to this projective proclivity, we can end up as moved by a Hepworth sculpture as we are by a more literal picture of maternal tenderness, for to our

Barbara Hepworth, *Two Segments and a Sphere*, 1936

inner eyes, there need be no difference between the expressive capacity of a representational painting and that of an arrangement of stones.

Secondly, our reasons for liking abstract sculptures, and by extension tables and columns, are not in the end so far removed from our reasons for honouring representational scenes. We call works in both genres beautiful when they succeed in evoking what seem to us the most attractive, significant attributes of human beings and animals.

5.

Once we start to look, we will find no shortage of suggestions of living forms in the furniture and houses around us. There are penguins in our water jugs and stout and self-important personages in our kettles, graceful deer in our desks and oxen in our dining-room tables.

A weary, sceptical eye gazes out at us from the roof of Alfred Messel's Wertheim Department Store in Berlin, while upturned insect legs guard the Castel Béranger in Paris. An aggressive beetle lurks in Malaysia's Putrajaya Convention Centre and a warmer, hedgehog-related creature in the Sage Arts Centre in Gateshead.

Hedgehogs, beetles, eyes and legs:
Clockwise from top left: Foster and Partners, Sage Arts Centre, Gateshead, 2005
Hijjas Kasturi, Convention Centre, Putrajaya, 2003
Alfred Messel, Wertheim Department Store, Berlin, 1904
Hector Guimard, Castel Béranger, Paris, 1896

Even in something as diminutive as the letters of a typeface, we may detect well-developed personalities, about whose lives and daydreams we could without great difficulty write a short story. The straight back and alert upright bearing of a Helvetican 'f' hint at a punctual, clean and optimistic protagonist, whereas his Poliphilus cousin, with a droopy head and soft features, strikes a sleepier, more sheepish and more pensive note. The story may not end well for him.

Helvetica   Poliphilus

In a kitchenware shop may be found an equally vivid assortment of types. Stemmed glasses seem generically feminine, though this category nonetheless encompasses warm-hearted matrons, nymphets and nervy blue-stockings, while the more masculine tumblers count among their number lumberjacks and stern civil servants.

The tradition of equating furniture and buildings with living beings can be traced back to the Roman author Vitruvius, who paired each of the three principal classical orders with a human or divine archetype from Greek mythology. The Doric column, with its plain capital and squat profile, had its equivalent in the muscular, martial hero Hercules; the Ionic column, with its decorated scrolls and base, corresponded with the stolid, middle-aged goddess Hera; and the Corinthian column, the most intricately embellished of the three and the one with the tallest, slenderest profile, found its model in the beautiful adolescent deity Aphrodite.

In homage to Vitruvius, we might pass the time on car journeys aligning the pillars of motorway bridges to appropriate bipedal counterparts. A drive might reveal a sedentary and cheerful woman holding up one bridge, a punctilious, nervous accountant with an authoritarian air supporting another.

If we can judge the personality of objects from apparently minuscule features (a change of a few degrees in the angle of the rim can shift a wine glass from modesty to arrogance), it is because we first acquire this skill in relation to humans, whose characters we can impute from microscopic aspects of their skin tissue and muscle. An eye will move from implying apology to suggesting self-righteousness by way of a movement that is in a mechanical sense implausibly small. The width of a coin separates a brow that we take to be concerned from one that appears concentrated, or a mouth that implies sulkiness from one that suggests grief. Codifying such infinitesimal variations was the life's work of the Swiss pseudoscientist Johann Kaspar Lavater, whose four-volume *Essays on Physiognomy* (1783) analysed almost every conceivable connotation of facial features and supplied line drawings of an exhaustive array of chins, eye sockets, foreheads, mouths and noses, with interpretative adjectives appended to each illustration.

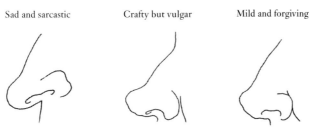

Sad and sarcastic   Crafty but vulgar   Mild and forgiving

What faces mean:
Johann Kaspar Lavater, *Essays on Physiognomy*, 1783

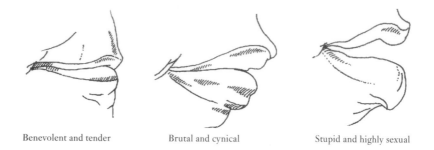

Benevolent and tender   Brutal and cynical   Stupid and highly sexual

The wealth of information we are attuned to deducing from living forms helps to explain the intensity of feelings generated by competing architectural styles. When only a millimetre separates a lethargic set of the mouth from a benevolent one, it is understandable that a great deal should seem to hang on the differing shapes of two windows or roof lines. It is natural for us to be as discriminating about the meanings of the objects we live among as we are about the faces of the people we spend time with.

To feel that a building is unappealing may simply be to dislike the temperament of the creature or human we dimly recognise in its elevation – just as to call another edifice beautiful is to sense the presence of a character we would like if it took on a living form. What we search for in a work of architecture is not in the end so far from what we search for in a friend. The objects we describe as beautiful are versions of the people we love.

Who would we want to be friends with?

6.

Even when objects don't look anything like people, we can find it easy to imagine what kinds of human characters they might have.

So refined is our skill at detecting parallels to human beings in forms, textures and colours that we can interpret a character from the humblest shape. A line is eloquent enough. A straight example will signal someone stable and dull, a wavy one will appear foppish and calm, and a jagged one angry and confused.

Consider the struts on the backs of two chairs. Both seem to express a mood. The curved struts speak of ease and playfulness, the straight ones of seriousness and logic. And yet neither set approximates a human shape. Rather, the struts abstractly represent two different temperaments. A straight piece of wood behaves in its own medium as a stable, unimaginative person will act in his or her life, while the meanders of a curved piece correspond, however obliquely, with the casual elegance of an unruffled and dandyish soul.

The ease with which we can connect the psychological world with the outer, visual and sensory one seeds our language with metaphors. We can speak of someone being twisted or dark, smooth or hard. We can develop a steely heart or fall into a blue mood. We can compare a person to a material like concrete or a colour like burgundy and be sure thereby to convey something of his or her personality.

The German psychologist Rudolf Arnheim once asked his students to describe a good and a bad marriage using only line drawings. Although we might be hard pressed, working backwards, to divine Arnheim's brief from the ensuing squiggles, we could come close, for they are strikingly successful at capturing something of the qualities of two different kinds of relationship. In one example, smooth curves mirror the peaceable and flowing course of a loving union, while violently gyrating spikes serve as a visual shorthand for sarcastic putdowns and slammed doors.

Two stories about married life from Rudolf Arnheim, *Visual Thinking*, 1969

If even crude scratches on a piece of paper can speak accurately and fluently of our psychic states, when whole buildings are at stake, expressive potential is exponentially increased. The pointed arches of Bayeux Cathedral convey ardour and intensity, while their rounded counterparts in the courtyard of the Ducal Palace in Urbino embody serenity and poise. Like a person weathering life's challenges, the palace's arches equitably resist pressure from all sides, avoiding the spiritual crises and emotional effusions to which the cathedral's appear ineluctably drawn.

Contrasting temperaments:
Left: Ducal Palace, Urbino, 1479; right: Bayeux Cathedral, 1077

If, to take Arnheim's exercise several steps further, we were tasked with producing metaphoric images of Germany in two periods of her history, as a fascist state and a democratic republic, and if we were allowed to work with stone, steel and glass rather than with just a pencil, it is likely we could not better the iconic designs of Albert Speer and Egon Eiermann, who created national pavilions for World's Fairs on either side of the Second World War. Speer's offering, for the Paris Fair of 1937, makes use of the quintessential visual metaphors of power: height, mass and shadow. Without even laying eyes on the insignia of the government which sponsored it, we would almost certainly sense something ominous, aggressive and defiant emanating from this 500-foot Neoclassical colossus. Twenty-one years and a world war later, in his German Pavilion for the 1958 World Exposition in Brussels, Egon Eiermann would resort to a

trio of very different metaphors: horizontality to suggest calm, lightness to imply gentleness and transparency to evoke democracy.

So eloquent are materials and colours, then, that a façade can be made to speak of how a country should be ruled and which principles ought to govern its foreign policy. Political and ethical ideas can be written into window frames and door handles. An abstract glass box on a stone plinth can deliver a paean to tranquillity and civilisation.

7.

There is yet a third way in which objects and buildings communicate meaning, one we might begin to get a feel for if we were invited to dinner at the German Ambassador's in Washington, DC. Sited on a wooded hill in the north-western section of the capital, the residence is an imposing structure with a formal and Classical air, its outer walls clad in white limestone and its interiors dominated by marble floors, oak doors, and leather and steel furniture. Ushered out onto the veranda for a prepandial glass of sparkling Rhine wine and a cocktail sausage, we would – given a relevant historical awareness – see something so unexpected and shocking that we could only gasp as our impeccably polite hosts pointed out features of the skyline in their flawless English. It would not be the silhouettes of the city's landmarks, however, that occasioned our astonishment but rather the portico itself, whispering in our ears of torch-lit parades, military processions and martial salutes. In both its dimensions and its forms, the rear elevation of the German Ambassador's Residence bears an uncanny likeness to Albert Speer's ambulatory at the Nuremberg Parade Ground.

Insofar as buildings speak to us, they also do so through quotation – that is, by referring to, and triggering memories of, the contexts in which we have previously seen them, their counterparts or their models. They communicate by prompting associations. We seem incapable of looking

Top: Albert Speer, German Pavilion, World's Fair, Paris, 1937
Bottom: Egon Eiermann, Pavilion of the Federal Republic of Germany,
World Exposition, Brussels, 1958

Left: Albert Speer, ambulatory, Zeppelinfeld, Nuremberg, 1939
Right: Oswald Matthias Ungers, Residence of the German Ambassador, Washington, DC, 1995

at buildings or pieces of furniture without tying them to the historical and personal circumstances of our viewing; as a result, architectural and decorative styles become, for us, emotional souvenirs of the moments and settings in which we came across them.

So attentive are our eyes and our brains that the tiniest detail can unleash memories. The swollen-bellied 'B' or open-jawed 'G' of an Art Deco font is enough to inspire reveries of short-haired women with melon hats and posters advertising holidays in Palm Beach and Le Touquet.

ABCDEFGHIJKLMNOPQRSTUVWXYZ

Just as a childhood can be released from the odour of a washing powder or cup of tea, an entire culture can spring from the angles of a few lines. A steeply sloping tiled roof can at once engender thoughts of the English Arts and Crafts movement, while a gambrel-shaped one can as rapidly prompt memories of Swedish history and holidays on the archipelago south of Stockholm.

Left: C. F. A. Voysey, Moorcrag, Cumbria, 1899
Right: Stallarholmen, near Mariefred, Sweden, c. 1850

Walking past the Carlton Cinema on London's Essex Road, we may remark something oddly Egyptian about the windows. This stylistic term will occur to us because at some point in our past – perhaps on an evening when we watched a documentary about Ancient Egypt while eating dinner – our eyes took note of the angles of the pylon gateways to the temples at Karnak, Luxor and Philae. That we can now retrieve that half-forgotten detail and apply it to the narrowing of a city window is testament to the synaptic process by which our subconscious can master information and make connections that our conscious selves may be wholly incapable of articulating.

Left: Temple of Isis, Philae, c. 140 BC
Right: George Cole, Carlton Cinema, Essex Road, London, 1930

Relying on our associative powers, architects can dimple their arches and windows and feel confident that they will be understood as references to Islam. They can line their corridors with unpainted wooden planks and dependably allude to the rustic and the unpretentious. They can install thick white railings around balconies and know that their seaside villas will speak of ocean liners and the nautical life.

A more disturbing aspect of associations lies in their arbitrary nature, in the way they can lead us to pass a verdict on objects or buildings for reasons unconnected to their specifically architectural virtues or vices. We may make a judgement based on what they symbolise rather than on what they are.

We may decide that we hate nineteenth-century Gothic, for instance, because it characterised a house in which we were unhappy at university, or revile Neoclassicism (as exemplified by the German Ambassador's Residence or by the work of the architect Karl Friedrich Schinkel) because it had the misfortune to be favoured by the Nazis.

For proof of the capriciousness with which architectural and artistic styles fall victim to baleful associations, we need only note that, in most cases, little besides time is required for them to recover their charm. The remove of a few generations or more allows us to regard objects or buildings without the biases which entrammel almost every era. With the passage of time, we can gaze at a seventeenth-century statuette of the Virgin Mary untroubled by images of overzealous Jesuits or the fires of the Inquisition. With time, we can accept and love Rococo detailing on its own terms, rather than seeing it as a mere symbol of aristocratic decadence cut short by revolutionary vengeance. With time, we may even be able to stand on the veranda of the German Ambassador's Residence and admire the proud, bold forms of its portico without being haunted by visions of storm troopers and torch-lit processions.

We might define genuinely beautiful objects as those endowed with sufficient innate assets as to withstand our positive or negative projections. They embody good qualities rather than simply remind us of them. They can thus outlive their temporal or geographic origins and communicate their intentions long after their initial audiences have disappeared. They can assert their attributes over and above the ebb and flow of our unfairly generous or damning associations.

8.

Despite the expressive potential of objects and buildings, discussion of what they talk about remains rare. We appear to feel more comfortable contemplating historical sources and stylistic tropes than we do delving into anthropomorphic, metaphoric or evocative meanings. It remains odd to initiate a conversation about what a building is saying.

We might find such activities easier if architectural features were more explicitly connected with their utterances – if there existed a dictionary, for example, which systematically correlated media and forms with emotions and ideas. Such a dictionary would most helpfully supply analyses of materials (of aluminium and steel, of terracotta and concrete) as well as of styles and dimensions (of every conceivable roof angle and every thickness and type of column). It would include paragraphs on the significance of convex and concave lines, and of reflective and plain glass.

The dictionary would resemble the giant catalogues which provide architects with information on light fittings and ironmongery, but, rather than focusing as those do on mechanical performance and compliance with building codes, it would expound on the expressive implications of every element in an architectural composition.

In its comprehensive concern with minutiae, the dictionary would acknowledge the fact that just as the alteration of a single word can change the whole sense of a poem, so, too, can our impression of a house be transformed when a straight limestone lintel is exchanged for a fractionally curved brick one. With the aid of such a resource, we might become more conscious readers, as well as writers, of our environment.

9.

As useful as such a handbook might be, however, in annotating what architecture talks to us about, it would not on its own ever be able to explain what it is about certain buildings that makes them appear to speak *beautifully*.

The buildings we admire are ultimately those which, in a variety of ways, extol values we think worthwhile – which refer, that is, whether through their materials, shapes or colours, to such legendarily positive qualities as friendliness, kindness, subtlety, strength and intelligence. Our sense of beauty and our understanding of the nature of a good life are intertwined. We seek associations of peace in our bedrooms, metaphors for generosity and harmony in our chairs, and an air of honesty and forth-rightness in our taps. We can be moved by a column that meets a roof with grace, by worn stone steps that hint at wisdom and by a Georgian doorway that demonstrates playfulness and courtesy in its fanlight window.

It was Stendhal who offered the most crystalline expression of the intimate affiliation between visual taste and our values when he wrote, 'Beauty is the promise of happiness.' His aphorism has the virtue of differentiating our love of beauty from an academic preoccupation with aesthetics, and integrating it instead with the qualities we need to prosper as whole human beings. If the search for happiness is the underlying quest of our lives, it seems only natural that it should simultaneously be the essential theme to which beauty alludes.

But because Stendhal was sensitive to the complexity of our require-ments for happiness, he wisely refrained from specifying any particular type of beauty. As individuals we may, after all, find vanity no less attrac-tive than graciousness, or aggression as intriguing as respect. Through

A promise of playfulness and courtesy:
Thomas Leverton, fanlight window, Bedford Square, 1783

his use of the capacious word 'happiness', Stendhal allowed for the wide range of goals which people have pursued. Understanding that mankind would always be as conflicted about its visual tastes as about its ethical ones, he noted, 'There are as many styles of beauty as there are visions of happiness.'

To call a work of architecture or design beautiful is to recognise it as a rendition of values critical to our flourishing, a transubstantiation of our individual ideals in a material medium.

Every architectural style speaks of an understanding of happiness:
John Pardey, Duckett House, New Forest, 2004

IV. Ideals of Home

1.

If it is true that the buildings and furnishings which we describe as beautiful evoke aspects of happiness, we might nevertheless ask why we find such evocation to be necessary. It is easy enough to understand why we would want such qualities as dignity and clarity to play a role in our lives; less clear is why we should also need the objects around us to speak to us of them. Why should it matter what our environment has to say to us? Why should architects bother to design buildings which communicate specific sentiments and ideas, and why should we be so negatively affected by places which reverberate with what we take to be the wrong allusions? Why are we vulnerable, so inconveniently vulnerable, to what the spaces we inhabit are saying?

2.

Our sensitivity to our surroundings may be traced back to a troubling feature of human psychology: to the way we harbour within us many different selves, not all of which feel equally like 'us', so much so that in certain moods, we can complain of having come adrift from what we judge to be our true selves.

Unfortunately, the self we miss at such moments, the elusively authentic, creative and spontaneous side of our character, is not ours to summon at will. Our access to it is, to a humbling extent, determined by the places we happen to be in, by the colour of the bricks, the height of the ceilings and the layout of the streets. In a hotel room strangled by three motorways, or in a waste land of run-down tower blocks, our optimism and sense of purpose are liable to drain away, like water from a punctured container. We may start to forget that we ever had ambitions or reasons to feel spirited and hopeful.

We depend on our surroundings obliquely to embody the moods and ideas we respect and then to remind us of them. We look to our buildings to hold us, like a kind of psychological mould, to a helpful vision of ourselves. We arrange around us material forms which communicate to us what we need – but are at constant risk of forgetting we need – within. We turn to wallpaper, benches, paintings and streets to staunch the disappearance of our true selves.

In turn, those places whose outlook matches and legitimates our own, we tend to honour with the term 'home'. Our homes do not have to offer us permanent occupancy or store our clothes to merit the name. To speak of home in relation to a building is simply to recognise its harmony with our own prized internal song. Home can be an airport or a library, a garden or a motorway diner.

Our love of home is in turn an acknowledgement of the degree to which our identity is not self-determined. We need a home in the psychological sense as much as we need one in the physical: to compensate for a vulnerability. We need a refuge to shore up our states of mind, because so much of the world is opposed to our allegiances. We need our rooms to align us to desirable versions of ourselves and to keep alive the important, evanescent sides of us.

3.

It is the world's great religions that have perhaps given most thought to the role played by the environment in determining identity and so – while seldom constructing places where we might fall asleep – have shown the greatest sympathy for our need for a home.

The very principle of religious architecture has its origins in the notion that where we are critically determines what we are able to believe in. To defenders of religious architecture, however convinced we are at an intellectual level of our commitments to a creed, we will remain reliably devoted to it only when it is continually affirmed by our buildings. In danger of being corrupted by our passions and led astray by the commerce and chatter of our societies, we require places where the values outside of us encourage and enforce the aspirations within us. We may be nearer or further away from God on account of what is represented on the walls or the ceilings. We need panels of gold and lapis, windows of coloured glass and gardens of immaculately raked gravel in order to stay true to the sincerest parts of ourselves.

4.

A few years ago, caught out by a heavy downpour, with a couple of hours to kill after being stood up for lunch by a friend, I took shelter in a smoked glass and granite block on London's Victoria Street, home to the Westminster branch of McDonald's. The mood inside the restaurant was solemn and concentrated. Customers were eating alone, reading papers or staring at the brown tiles, masticating with a sternness and brusqueness beside which the atmosphere of a feeding shed would have appeared convivial and mannered.

The setting served to render all kinds of ideas absurd: that human beings might sometimes be generous to one another without hope of reward; that relationships can on occasion be sincere; that life may be worth enduring… The restaurant's true talent lay in the generation of anxiety. The harsh lighting, the intermittent sounds of frozen fries being sunk into vats of oil and the frenzied behaviour of the counter staff invited thoughts of the loneliness and meaninglessness of existence in a random and violent universe. The only solution was to continue to eat in an attempt to compensate for the discomfort brought on by the location in which one was doing so.

However, my meal was disturbed by the arrival of thirty or so implausibly tall and blond Finnish teenagers. The shock of finding themselves so far south and of exchanging glacial snow for mere rain had lent them extremely high spirits, which they expressed by unsheathing straws, bursting into ardent song and giving one another piggy-back rides – to the confusion of the restaurant staff, who were uncertain whether to condemn such behaviour or to respect it as a promise of voracious appetites.

Prompted by the voluble Finns to draw my visit to a precipitate close, I cleared my table and walked out into the plaza immediately adjacent to the restaurant, where I properly noticed for the first time the incongruous and imposing Byzantine forms of Westminster Cathedral, its red and white brick campanile soaring eighty-seven metres into the foggy London skies.

Drawn by rain and curiosity, I entered a cavernous hall, sunk in tarry darkness, against which a thousand votive candles stood out, their golden shadows flickering over mosaics and carved representations of the Stations of the Cross. There were smells of incense and sounds of murmured prayer. Hanging from the ceiling at the centre of the nave was a ten-metre-high crucifix, with Jesus on one side and his mother on the other. Around the high altar, a mosaic showed Christ enthroned in the heavens, encircled by angels, his feet resting on a globe, his hands clasping a chalice overflowing with his own blood.

The facile din of the outer world had given way to awe and silence. Children stood close to their parents and looked around with an air of puzzled reverence. Visitors instinctively whispered, as if deep in some collective dream from which they did not wish to emerge. The anonymity of the street had here been subsumed by a peculiar kind of intimacy. Everything serious in human nature seemed to be called to the surface: thoughts about limits and infinity, about powerlessness and sublimity. The stonework threw into relief all that was compromised and dull, and kindled a yearning for one to live up to its perfections.

After ten minutes in the cathedral, a range of ideas that would have been inconceivable outside began to assume an air of reasonableness. Under

What can we believe where?
Left: Elsom, Pack and Roberts Architects, McDonald's,
Ashdown House, Victoria Street, London, 1975
Right: John Francis Bentley, the nave, Westminster Cathedral, London, 1903

the influence of the marble, the mosaics, the darkness and the incense, it seemed entirely probable that Jesus was the son of God and had walked across the Sea of Galilee. In the presence of alabaster statues of the Virgin Mary set against rhythms of red, green and blue marble, it was no longer surprising to think that an angel might at any moment choose to descend through the layers of dense London cumulus, enter through a window in the nave, blow a golden trumpet and make an announcement in Latin about a forthcoming celestial event.

Concepts that would have sounded demented forty metres away, in the company of a party of Finnish teenagers and vats of frying oil, had succeeded – through a work of architecture – in acquiring supreme significance and majesty.

5.

The first attempts to create specifically Christian spaces, buildings intended to help their occupants to draw closer to the truths of the Gospels, date from some 200 years after the birth of Christ. On plaster walls in low-ceilinged, candlelit rooms, beneath the heathen streets of Rome, untrained artists painted crude renditions of incidents in Jesus's life, in a primitive style which might have done justice to the less gifted students of an art school.

The Breaking of the Bread, Catacomb of Priscilla, Rome, third century AD

These Christian catacombs are only the more touching, however, for their inarticulacy. They show the architectural and artistic impulses in their purest forms, without the elaboration supplied by talent or money. They reveal how in the absence of great patrons or craftsmen, with no skills or resources to speak of, the faithful will feel a need to daub the symbols of their heavens on damp cellar walls – to ensure that what is around them will fortify the truths within them.

From AD 379, when the Emperor Theodosius the Great declared Christianity the official religion of Rome, church architects were free to create homes for their ideals on a grander scale. Their aspirations achieved an apotheosis during the age of the cathedrals, in giant jewels of stone and glass designed to make vivid the Paradise of the holy books.

In the eyes of medieval man, a cathedral was God's house on earth. Adam's fall might have obscured the true order of the cosmos, rendering most of the world sinful and irregular, but within the bounds of a cathedral, the original, geometric beauty of the Garden of Eden had been resurrected. The light shining through the stained-glass windows prefigured that which would radiate in the next life. Inside the holy cavern, the claims of the Book of Revelation ceased to seem remote and bizarre, and became instead both palpable and immediate.

Touring the cathedrals today with cameras and guidebooks in hand, we may experience something at odds with our practical secularism: a peculiar and embarrassing desire to fall to our knees and worship a being as mighty and sublime as we ourselves are small and inadequate. Such a reaction would not, of course, have surprised the cathedral builders, for it was precisely towards such a surrender of our self-sufficiency that their efforts were directed, the purpose of their ethereal walls and lace-like ceilings being to make metaphysical stirrings not only plausible but irresistible within even the soberest of hearts.

Opposite: west front, Reims Cathedral, after 1254

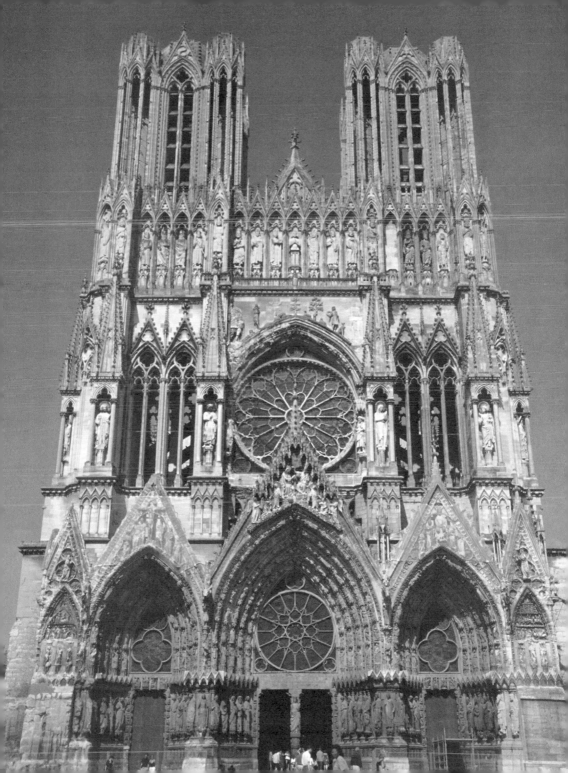

6.

The architects and artists who worked in the service of early Islam were likewise driven by the wish to create a physical backdrop which would bolster the claims of their religion. Holding that God was the source of all understanding, Islam placed particular emphasis on the divine qualities of mathematics. Muslim artisans covered the walls of houses and mosques with repeating sequences of delicate and complicated geometries, through which the infinite wisdom of God might be intimated. This ornamentation, so pleasingly intricate on a rug or a cup, was nothing less than hallucinatory when applied to an entire hall. Eyes accustomed to seeing only the practical and humdrum objects of daily life could, inside such a room, survey a world shorn of all associations with the everyday. They would sense a symmetry, without quite being able to grasp its underlying logic. Such works were like the products of a mind with none of our human limitations, of a higher power untainted by human coarseness and therefore worthy of unconditional reverence.

Islamic architects wrote their religion literally as well as symbolically onto their buildings. The corridors of the Nasrid kings' Alhambra Palace displayed quotations from the holy texts, carved on panels in a floriated Kufic script. 'In the name of the merciful God. He is God alone, God entire. He has neither begotten, nor is He begotten. And none is His equal,' read one hymn which wrapped around a reception room at eye level. In the main chamber of the complex's Torre de la Cautiva hung a panel featuring letters threaded through with geometric and vegetal shapes in patterns of phosphorescent complexity. *Al-mulk li-llah* ('Power belongs to God'), declared the wall, the strokes of the letters prolonged so as to form semicircular arches which divided, crossed and then intersected with the limbs of a second inscription proclaiming, *Al-'izz li-llah* ('Glory belongs to God') – word and image consummately united to remind onlookers of the purpose of Islamic existence.

Top: cupola of the Mausoleum of Turabeg Khanum, Kunya, Urgench, 1370
Bottom: ceramic tiles, The Alcazar, Seville, fourteenth century

7.

In both early Christianity and Islam, theologians made a claim about architecture likely to sound so peculiar to modern ears as to be worthy of sustained examination: they proposed that beautiful buildings had the power to improve us morally and spiritually. They believed that, rather than corrupting us, rather than being an idle indulgence for the decadent, exquisite surroundings could edge us towards perfection. A beautiful building could reinforce our resolve to be good.

Behind this distinctive claim lay another astonishing belief: that of an equivalence between the visual and the ethical realms. Attractive architecture was held to be a version of goodness in a non-verbal idiom – and its ugly counterpart, a material version of evil. Thus, a plainly sculpted door handle which pleased us through its simplicity could simultaneously function as a reminder of the virtues of sobriety and moderation, just as the delicate setting of a pane of glass within a window frame could covertly deliver a sermon on the theme of gentleness.

The moral equation between beauty and goodness lent to all architecture a new seriousness and importance. In admiring the noble patina of a mature wooden floor, we would – after all – no longer merely be delighting in a piece of interior decoration. We would be taking in a lesson in righteousness.

We might even, the early theologians suggested, come better to understand God through beauty, for it was He who had created every beautiful thing in the world: the eastern sky at dawn, the forests, the animals, and even more domestic items like a graceful armchair, a bowl of lemons and a ray of afternoon sun shining through a cotton window blind onto the kitchen table. In contact with attractive buildings, we could intimate some of the refinement, intelligence, kindness and harmony of their ultimate maker. In the eleventh century the Muslim philosopher Ibn Sina noted

Opposite: Ibn al-Jayyāb, decorative plaster panel, main room,
Torre de la Cautiva, Alhambra Palace, c. 1340
Al-mulk li-llah = Power belongs to God; Al-'izz li-llah = Glory belongs to God

that to admire a mosaic for being flawless, ordered and symmetrical, was at the same time to recognise divine glory, for 'God is at the source of every beautiful thing.' In the thirteenth century, from across a divide of faith, Robert Grosseteste, Bishop of Lincoln, asked us to picture 'a beautiful house, this beautiful universe. Think of this or that beautiful object. But then, omitting "this" and "that", think of what makes "this" and "that" beautiful. Try to see what Beauty is in itself… If you succeed, you will see God Himself, the Beauty which dwells in all beautiful things.'

A second compelling claim was made for the visual when the early theologians speculated that it might be easier to become a faithful servant of God by *looking* than by *reading*. They argued that mankind could more effectively be shaped by architecture than by Scripture. Because we were creatures of sense, spiritual principles stood a better chance of fortifying our souls if we took them in via our eyes rather than via our intellect. We might learn more about humility by gazing at an arrangement of tiles than by studying the Gospels, and more about the nature of kindness in a stained-glass window than in a holy book. Spending time in beautiful spaces, far from a self-indulgent luxury, was deemed to lie at the core of the quest to become an honorable person.

8.
Secular architecture may have no clearly defined ideology to defend, no sacred text to quote from and no god to worship, but, just like its religious counterpart, it possesses the power to shape those who come within its orbit. The gravity with which religions have at points treated the decoration of their surroundings invites us to lend equal significance to the decoration of profane places, for they, too, may offer the better parts of us a home.

Advocates of the pursuit of architectural beauty, whether secular or religious, ultimately justify their ambitions through an appeal to the same phenomenon: man's inability to flourish in equal measure in whatever room he is placed in.

The challenge facing ordinary home-builders is no different from that which faced the architects of Chartres and the mosque of Masjid-I Imam in Isfahan, even if their budgets are closer to those of the painters of the Roman catacombs. In a secular context, too, our aim is to identify objects and decorative features which will correlate with certain salutary inner states and encourage us to foster them within ourselves.

9.

Imagine being able to return at the close of each day to a house like that in Rö, north of Stockholm. Our working routines may be frantic and compromised, dense with meetings, insincere handshakes, small-talk and bureaucracy. We may say things we don't believe in to win over our colleagues and feel ourselves becoming envious and excited in relation to goals we don't essentially care for.

But, finally, on our own, looking out of the hall window onto the garden and the gathering darkness, we can slowly resume contact with a more authentic self, who was there waiting in the wings for us to end our performance. Our submerged playful sides will derive encouragement from the painted flowers on either side of the door. The value of gentleness will be confirmed by the delicate folds of the curtains. Our interest in a modest, tender-hearted kind of happiness will be fostered by the unpretentious raw wooden floorboards. The materials around us will speak to us of the highest hopes we have for ourselves. In this setting, we can come close to a state of mind marked by integrity and vitality. We can feel inwardly liberated. We can, in a profound sense, return home.

Without honouring any gods, a piece of domestic architecture, no less than a mosque or a chapel, can assist us in the commemoration of our genuine selves.

Näs House, Rö, north of Stockholm, *c.* 1820

10.

Just like an entire room, a single picture can assist us in recovering the lost, significant parts of ourselves.

Take William Nicholson's closely observed painting of a bowl, a white tablecloth and some unshelled peas. On first seeing it, we might experience a measure of sadness, as we recognise how far we have drifted from its meditative, observant spirit, from its modesty and appreciation of the beauty and nobility of ordinary life.

Behind wanting to own the painting and hang it where we could regularly study it might be the hope that through continued exposure to it, its qualities would come to assume a greater hold on us. Passing it on the stairs last thing at night or in the morning on our way to work would have the effect of a magnet which could pull to the surface submerged filaments of our characters. The painting would act as the guardian of a mood.

We value certain buildings for their ability to rebalance our misshapen natures and encourage emotions which our predominant commitments force us to sacrifice. Feelings of competitiveness, envy and aggression hardly need elaboration, but feelings of humility amid an immense and sublime universe, of a desire for calm at the onset of evening or of an aspiration for gravity and kindness – these form no correspondingly reliable part of our inner landscape, a rueful absence which may explain our wish to bind such emotions to the fabric of our homes.

Architecture can arrest transient and timid inclinations, amplify and solidify them, and thereby grant us more permanent access to a range of emotional textures which we might otherwise have experienced only accidentally and occasionally.

There need be nothing preternaturally sweet or homespun about the moods embodied in domestic spaces. These spaces can speak to us of the sombre as readily as they can of the gentle. There is no necessary

William Nicholson, *The Lustre Bowl with Green Peas*, 1911

connection between the concepts of home and of prettiness; what we call a home is merely any place that succeeds in making more consistently available to us the important truths which the wider world ignores, or which our distracted and irresolute selves have trouble holding on to.

As we write, so we build: to keep a record of what matters to us.

11.

Given the memorial capacities of architecture, it cannot be coincidental that in many of the world's cultures, the earliest and most significant works have been funerary.

Some 4,000 years ago, on a hillside in western Pembrokeshire, a group of our Neolithic ancestors lifted up a series of gigantic stones with their bare hands and covered them with earth to mark the spot where one of their kinsmen lay buried. The chamber has been lost to time, as have the body and even the identity of the man whose name must once have been spoken with awe in the communities along this damp edge of the British Isles. But what remains to these stones is their eloquent ability to deliver the message common to all funerary architecture, from marble tomb to rough wooden roadside shrine – namely, 'Remember'. The poignancy of the roughly chiselled family of mossy orthostats, keeping their lonely watch over a landscape around which none save sheep and the occasional rain-proofed hiker now roam, is heightened only by the awareness that we recall nothing whatsoever about the one they memorialise – aside, that is, from this leader's evident desire, strong enough to inspire his clan to raise a forty-tonne capstone in his honour, that he not be forgotten.

The fear of forgetting anything precious can trigger in us the wish to raise a structure, like a paperweight to hold down our memories. We might even follow the example of the Countess of Mount Edgcumbe, who in the late eighteenth century had a thirty-foot-high Neoclassical obelisk erected on a hill on the outskirts of Plymouth, in memory of an

Top: Neolithic burial chamber, Pentre Ifan, western Pembrokeshire, c. 2000 BC
Opposite: Memorial to Cupid, Plymouth, c. 1790

unusually sensitive pig called Cupid, whom she did not hesitate to call a true friend.

The desire to remember unites our reasons for building for the living and for the dead. As we put up tombs, markers and mausoleums to memorialise lost loved ones, so do we construct and decorate buildings to help us recall the important but fugitive parts of ourselves. The pictures and chairs in our homes are the equivalents – scaled for our own day, attuned to the demands of the living – of the giant burial mounds of Palaeolithic times. Our domestic fittings, too, are memorials to identity.

12.

We may occasionally and guiltily experience the desire to create a home as a wish to vaunt ourselves in front of others. But only if the truest parts of ourselves were egomaniacal would the urge to build be dominated by the need to boast. Instead, at its most genuine, the architectural impulse seems connected to a longing for communication and commemoration, a longing to declare ourselves to the world through a register other than words, through the language of objects, colours and bricks: an ambition to let others know who we are – and, in the process, to remind ourselves.

1.

In 1575 the city of Venice commissioned the artist Paolo Veronese to paint a new ceiling for the great hall in the Doge's Palace, the Sala del Collegio, where the magistracy held its deliberations, and where dignitaries and ambassadors were received.

The resulting work was a sumptuous celebration, in allegorical form, of Venetian government. In a central panel Veronese depicted the city as a sober, beautiful queen of the seas, attended by two ladies-in-waiting, one of whom symbolised justice (she was carrying a pair of scales) and the other peace (she had a sleepy but not unferocious-seeming lion on a leash – just in case). Smaller panels around the edges portrayed supplementary Venetian virtues. *Meekness* showed a young blonde with an obedient sheep resting its front feet on her lap. Next to her, in *Fidelity*, a melancholic brunette stroked the neck of a St Bernard. Across from these was *Prosperity*, represented by a ruddy-cheeked, slightly chubby woman in a low-cut dress, holding a cornucopia overflowing with apples, grapes and oranges. And opposite her was *Moderation*, in which a sturdy maiden with braided hair and one exposed breast smiled impassively as she plucked out the feathers of a vicious-looking eagle (most likely standing in for the Turks or the Spanish). To judge from Veronese's ceiling, there was little that was not just and peaceful, meek and faithful, about the Venetian Republic.

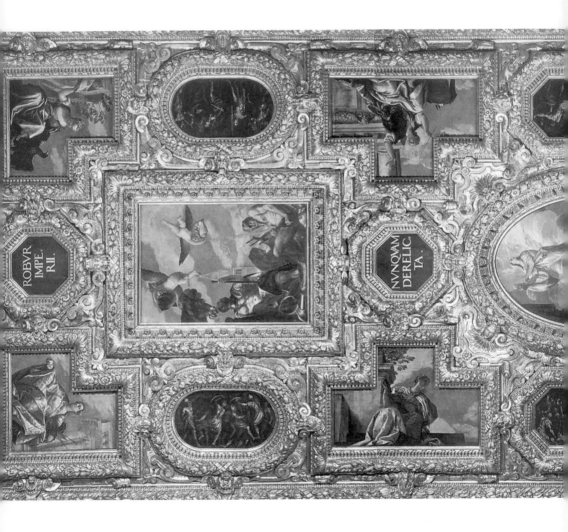

Previous page: Paolo Veronese, *Meekness*, Sala del Collegio, Doge's Palace, Venice, *c.* 1575
This page: Paolo Veronese, *The Triumph of Venice*, Sala del Collegio

Andrea Palladio, Villa Rotonda, Veneto, 1580

On a plot of land not many miles away, in 1566, a scholar, courtier and merchant named Canon Paolo Almerico asked Veronese's contemporary Andrea Palladio to build him a country house, to which he and his family might retreat to escape the intrigue and disease endemic to life on the republic's lagoons. Palladio was impressed by how well Ancient Roman buildings had managed to embody the ideals of their society – orderliness, courage, self-sacrifice and dignity – and he wanted his own designs to promote a comparable Renaissance conception of nobility. The title page of his 1570 work *The Four Books of Architecture* would make this didactic ambition explicit, through an allegorical engraving which featured two maidens of architecture saluting the queen of virtue. The balanced façades of the Villa Rotonda, the grand house which Palladio conceived for Almerico, seemed to imply that in this one place on earth, amid the sunlit flatlands of the Veneto, the struggles and compromises of ordinary life had been overcome and supplanted by equilibrium and lucidity. Along the villa's pediments and stairways, a sequence of life-sized statues by the sculptors Lorenzo Rubini and Giambattista Albanese gave human form to figures from classical mythology. Stepping out onto the terrace for a breath of air after reading a few chapters of Seneca or reviewing a contract from the Levant, the villa's owner could raise his eyes to take in Mercury, the protector of commerce, Jupiter, the god of wisdom, or Vesta, the goddess of the hearth – and feel that, in his country dwelling, at least, the values closest to his heart had found lasting expression and glorification in stone.

From Palladio's time forward, and due in large part to his example, the creation of houses which could reflect the ideals of their owners became a central ambition of architects throughout the West. In 1764 Lord Mansfield, England's Lord Chief Justice, tasked Robert Adam with coordinating the refurbishment of the library at Kenwood, his house on Hampstead Heath, overlooking London. Under Adam's direction, the library became an opulent consecration of the character of the most senior legal authority in the land. Its shelves were filled with volumes of Greek and Roman philosophy and history, and its ornate ceiling was inset with an allegorical oval. Entitled *Hercules between Glory and the Passions*, the vignette showed a young Hellenic hero, clearly a version of Mansfield himself, trying to decide whether to devote his life to pleasure (in the shape of three comely girls, one of whom was baring a plump thigh) or to follow the path of sacrifice to a worthy civic cause (personified by a soldier who pointed towards a Classical temple). The viewer was given to understand that civic virtue would win the tussle – though the painting, with its masterly Italianate command of flesh tones, seemed covertly to be making a more compelling case for the alternative. Another section of the ceiling displayed *Justice Embracing Peace, Commerce and Navigation* (it looked like a much-longed-for reunion), while over the fireplace hung a portrait of Lord Mansfield by David Martin, who had chosen – or been directed – to portray him leaning against the Temple of Solomon (the wisest of all the kings of Israel), under the approving gaze of a bust of Homer (the greatest of all storytellers), with his right hand holding open a volume of Cicero (the noblest orator). Here was a man of biblical, Greek and Roman sagacity.

Some sixty years later, just a few miles to the south, the members of London's Athenaeum Club, an institution catering (as its rulebook stated) to 'persons of distinguished eminence in science, literature, the arts or public life', commissioned a new building for themselves on Pall Mall. Classical figures, modelled after those in the Elgin Marbles and executed by the sculptor John Henning, were arranged on an extended frieze some 260 feet long, which wrapped around three exterior sides of the clubhouse. The figures were engaged in the Athenian equivalents of the activities which interested the English gentlemen inside: singing, reading, writing and orating. Above the front door stood a towering gilded statue of Athena. The goddess of craft and wisdom looked defiantly down Pall

Robert Adam, library, Kenwood House, 1769

Decimus Burton, Athenaeum Club, 1824; E. H. Bailey, *Athena*, 1829

Mall, intent on offering all who passed a foretaste of the personalities and interests of the membership within. By all appearances, only a few metres removed from the shallow commercialism of Piccadilly, an institution had been founded which harboured within its walls a group of men fully the equals of those who had lent glory to Athens in her golden age.

2.

Faced with painted ceilings and statues, in front of allegories of nymphs and gods, our eyes are liable to glaze over and drift away. The idealising style that in many countries dominated architecture between the six-teenth and nineteenth centuries has a habit of striking us as both tedious and hypocritical.

We find it hard to overlook, let alone forgive, the frequent discrepancies between idealised architecture and the reality of those who commissioned and lived with it. We know that Venice, whatever Veronese implied, repeatedly absconded from the virtues trumpeted by the maidens on the Sala del Collegio's ceiling. We know that she trafficked in slaves, ignored her poor, dissipated her resources and exacted immoderate revenge on her enemies. We know that La Serenissima painted one thing, and did another. We know, too, that the Almerico family fell into disgrace before Palladio's villa had even been completed and that their successors, the Capras, enjoyed no greater favour from the gods of commerce and wisdom, who seemed to mock the family's aspirations from the villa's rooftops. For his part, Lord Mansfield, far from uniting the talents of Cicero, Homer and Solomon, was an archetypal mid-eighteenth-century lawyer, ruthless, frugal with his humanity and adept at hiding his baser instincts behind Classical quotations. As for the Athenaeum, the majority of its members had joined the club for social advancement and wasted their days slumped in leather armchairs, watching the rain fall, slurping nursery food and neglecting their families, bearing as much resemblance to the contemporaries of Pericles as Piccadilly Circus did to the Acropolis.

By contrast with our idealising predecessors, we tend to pride ourselves on our interest in reality. We reward works of art precisely insofar as they leave roseate ideals behind and faithfully attune themselves to the facts of our condition. We honour these works for revealing to us who we are, rather than who we would like to be.

Nevertheless, the sheer eccentricity and remoteness of the concept of artistic idealisation invites closer examination. We might ask why, for some three centuries in the early-modern period, artists were applauded chiefly insofar as they could produce landscapes, people and buildings that were free of ordinary blemishes. We might wonder why artists competed among themselves to paint gardens and glades that would be more bucolic than any actual park, why they sculpted marble lips and ankles more seductive than those through which real blood might flow, and made portraits of aristocrats and royalty which showed them to be wiser and more magnanimous than they ever were.

It was rarely naivety that lay behind these efforts, or indeed the desire to deceive. The creators of idealised works were worldly creatures and credited their audiences with being so too. It was clear that the councillors gathering under Veronese's ceiling would frequently have been swayed by impulses darker than those depicted above them. Likewise, it was known that Mansfield's inclination to do honour to his office had to compete with the siren calls of wealth and fame, and that the hope of achieving something worthwhile over the course of an afternoon at the Athenaeum Club would seldom have withstood the lure of gossip and ginger biscuits in the tea room.

To proponents of the idealising tradition, the notion that artists were being naive in suggesting anything other than this would itself have appeared naive. The purpose of their art and their buildings was not to remind us of what life was typically like, but rather to keep before our eyes how it might optimally be, so as to move us fractionally closer to fulfilment and virtue. Sculptures and buildings were to assist us in bringing the best of ourselves to the fore. They were to embalm our highest aspirations.

3.

It is in German philosophy of the late eighteenth century that we find the most lucid articulations of the theory of artistic idealisation. In his *On the Aesthetic Education of Man* (1794), Friedrich Schiller proposed that the perfections presented in idealised art could be sources of inspiration, to which we would be able to turn when we had lost confidence in ourselves and were in contact only with our flaws, a melancholic and self-destructive stance to which he felt his own age especially prone. 'Humanity has lost its dignity,' he observed, 'but Art has rescued it and preserved it in significant stone. Truth lives on in the illusion of Art, and it is from this copy, or after-image, that the original image will once again be restored.'

Rather than confronting us with evocations of our darkest moments, works of art were to stand, in Schiller's words, as an 'absolute manifestation of potential'; they were to function like 'an escort descended from the world of the ideal'.

If buildings can act as a repository of our ideals, it is because they can be purged of all the infelicities that corrode ordinary lives. A great work of architecture will speak to us of a degree of serenity, strength, poise and grace to which we, both as creators and audiences, typically cannot do justice – and it will for this very reason beguile and move us. Architecture excites our respect to the extent that it surpasses us.

The potential inscribed in an idealised building need never fully be realised to justify its worth. In the eyes of Schiller's contemporary Wilhelm von Humboldt, it was the idealised buildings of the Ancient

An invitation to a Classical ideal:
Top: Karl Friedrich Schinkel, Schlossbrücke, Berlin, 1824; statue by Albert Wolff, 1853
Opposite: Karl Friedrich Schinkel, Altes Museum, Berlin, 1830

Greeks that presented modern Westerners with the most nourishing sources of inspiration, though he added in his essay 'Concerning the Study of Antiquity' (1793) that Greek architecture deserved our interest even if only a semblance of the perfections it alluded to could ever be re-created in the practically minded, bourgeois world: 'We imitate the models of the Greeks in full consciousness that they are unattainable; we fill our imagination with the images of their free, richly gained life, knowing that such life is denied us.'

When von Humboldt's friend, the architect Karl Friedrich Schinkel, began to endow Berlin with Classical bridges, museums and palaces, he knew that Berliners would only ever be able to admire from a distance, rather than rekindle, the antiquity he revered, but he trusted that something of the period's integrity and grandeur could through architecture still come to permeate the Prussian capital. As residents crossed the Schlossbrücke to attend a meeting or passed the New Pavilion at the

Charlottenhof Palace on a Sunday walk, Schinkel's architecture – his statue-laden bridges, his sober columns, his delicate frescos – could play a small but pivotal role in ushering in a renaissance of the spirit.

4.

However much it may seem as if we have lost all patience with idealisation, contemptuous as we are of decorated bridges and gilded statues, we are constitutionally incapable of abandoning the concept itself, for, freed of all its historical associations, the word 'idealisation' refers simply to an aspiration towards perfection, an objective with which no one, not even the most rational of beings, may ever be completely unacquainted.

It is in fact not ideals per se that we have forgone but the specific values once honoured by prominent works of idealisation. We have given up on antiquity, we have no reverence for mythology, and we condemn aristocratic confidence. Our ideals now revolve around themes of democracy, science and commerce. And yet we remain as committed as ever to the project of idealisation. Behind a practical façade, modern architecture has never ceased trying to reflect back to its audience a selective image of who they might be, in the hope of improving upon, and moulding, reality.

Idealising ambitions become especially evident whenever the construction of high-profile civic buildings is undertaken. The national pavilions of the World Exposition in Seville in 1992, for example, were in their understated way just as idealistic about their sponsoring countries as Veronese had been in his rendition of the virtues of Venetian government. Finland's entry, made up of two separate but conjoined halves – a polished steel slab nestling against a curved extension of blond wood – spoke of a society which had succeeded in perfectly reconciling the opposing elements of male and female, modernity and history, technology and nature, luxury and democracy. Taken as a whole, the ensemble comprised an austerely beautiful promise of a dignified and graceful life.

An ideal life in Finland: Left: Monark Architects, Finnish Pavilion, Expo '92, Seville, 1992
An ideal of a career in banking: Right: Frank Gehry, DZ Bank, Berlin, 2000

The workers of the DZ Bank in Berlin were offered a comparable version of an ideal by their headquarters beside the Brandenburg Gate. While their work itself might often be routine and repetitive, on their way to the cafeteria or a meeting, the bank's employees could look down into the giant atrium of their building at a strange, elegant conference room, whose lithe forms hinted at the creativity and playfulness to which their solemn bosses aspired.

Oscar Niemeyer, National Congress, Brasília, 1960

Entire cities may even be born out of the wish to summon Schiller's 'escort descended from the world of the ideal'. When President Kubitschek of Brazil unveiled plans for the construction of Brasília, in 1956, he vowed that the new capital would become 'the most original and precise expression of the creative intelligence of modern Brazil'. Deep and high in the country's interior, it was to be a model of modern bureaucratic efficiency, an ideal to which the rest of Kubitschek's sprawling, struggling country could pay only insecure and occasional homage. Brasília was intended not to symbolise an existing national reality but rather to bring a new reality into being. It was hoped that with its broad avenues and its undulating

Richard Neutra, Edgar J. Kaufmann House, Palm Springs, 1946

concrete and steel buildings, it would help erase Brazil's legacy of coloni-
alism, as well as the chaos and poverty of her coastal cities. Brasília would
bring about the modernity it epitomised. It would create a country in its
own image.

The fact that Brasília would end up having its share of beggars and
favelas, burnt grass on its spacious thoroughfares and cracks in the walls
of its cathedral, would not have dissuaded the champions of idealisation in architecture, any more than would betrayals and incompetence
beneath Veronese's ceiling, stupidity within the Athenaeum, alcoholism
and despair in Finland or terminal boredom in the offices of the DZ Bank.

For them, such lapses merely underscored the need for idealised forms to stand as a defence against all that remains corrupt and unimaginative within us.

In the modern age, idealisation has proved as attractive in the domestic sphere as in the civic one. The bourgeois couples who lived in Richard Neutra's mid-twentieth-century steel and glass pavilions in California may at times have drunk too much, squabbled, been insincere and overwhelmed by anxiety, but at least their buildings spoke to them of honesty and ease, of a lack of inhibition and a faith in the future – and would have reminded their owners, at the height of their tantrums or professional complications (when their fury rang out into the desert night), of what they longed for in their hearts.

In 1938, on a remote, rocky outcrop on the island of Capri, the Italian writer Curzio Malaparte conceived a home for himself which would be, as he wrote to a friend, 'a self-portrait in stone' ('ritratto pietra') and 'a house like me' ('una casa come me'). With its proud isolation, its juxtapositioning of ruggedness and refinement, its unblinking, hardy defiance of the elements, and the aesthetic debt it owed to Ancient Rome on the one hand and Italian modernism on the other, the house did indeed pick up on key traits of Malaparte's character. Fortunately for visitors, however, it turned out not to be a slavishly faithful portrait of its owner in all his facets – a difficult prospect for any house, certainly, but particularly so in Malaparte's case, for that would have necessitated the inclusion of pretentious furnishings, dead-end corridors, perhaps a shooting range (he was a Fascist until 1943) and a few broken windows (he liked a drink and then a fight). Rather than reflecting the author's many foibles, Casa Malaparte, like all effective works of idealisation, assisted its gifted yet flawed proprietor in orienting himself towards the noblest sides of his personality.

5.

The architecture produced under the influence of an idealising theory of the arts might be described as a form of propaganda. The word is an alarming one, for we are inclined to believe that high art should be free of ideology and admired purely for its own sake.

Yet the term 'propaganda' refers to the promotion of any doctrine or set of beliefs and in and of itself should carry no negative connotations. That the majority of such promotion has been in the service of odious political and commercial agendas is more an accident of history than any fault of the word. A work of art becomes a piece of propaganda whenever it uses its resources to direct us towards *something*, insofar as it attempts to enhance our sensitivity and our readiness to respond favourably to any end or idea.

A self-portrait in stone:
Curzio Malaparte (with Adalberto Libera), Casa Malaparte, Capri, 1943

Under this definition, few works of art could fail to be counted as propaganda: not only pictures of Soviet farmers proclaiming their five-year plans but also paintings of peas and lustre bowls; chairs; and steel and glass houses on the edge of the California desert. Taking the apparently perverse step of giving each of these the same label merely serves to stress the directive aspect of all consciously created objects – objects which invite viewers to imitate and participate in the qualities encoded within them.

From this perspective, we would be wise not to pursue the impossible goal of extirpating propaganda altogether, but should instead endeavour to surround ourselves with its more honourable examples. There is nothing to lament in the idea that art can direct our actions, provided that the directions it points us in are valuable ones. The theorists of the idealising tradition were refreshingly frank in their insistence that art should

John Wood the Younger, Royal Crescent, Bath, 1775

try to make things happen – and, more importantly, that it should try to make us good.

6.

A perplexing consequence of fixing our eyes on an ideal is that it may make us sad. The more beautiful something is, the sadder we risk feeling, so that standing in front of a painting by Pieter de Hooch of a grave-faced little boy diligently bringing his mother some loaves of bread, or of John Wood the Younger's Royal Crescent in Bath, we may find ourselves not so far from tears.

Our sadness won't be of the searing kind but more like a blend of joy and melancholy: joy at the perfection we see before us, melancholy at an awareness of how seldom we are sufficiently blessed to encounter anything of its kind. The flawless object throws into perspective the mediocrity that surrounds it. We are reminded of the way we would wish things always to be and of how incomplete our lives remain.

Pieter de Hooch, *A Boy Bringing Bread, c.* 1665

Pieter de Hooch's figures and the curve of the Royal Crescent stir us through the contrast they present to the emotions which more usually colour our days. The gentle manner of the mother and the trusting, dutiful expression of her son make us conscious of our own cynicism and brusqueness. The Royal Crescent, in all its solemn dignity, shows up the trivial and chaotic nature of so many of our ambitions. These works of art touch us because they are unlike us and yet also like the way we might wish ourselves to be.

Christian philosophers have been singularly alive to the sadness which beauty may provoke. 'When we admire the beauty of visible objects, we experience joy certainly,' observed the medieval thinker Hugh of St Victor, 'but at the same time, we experience a feeling of tremendous void.' The religious explanation put forward for this sadness, as rationally implausible as it is psychologically intriguing, is that we recognise beautiful things as symbols of the unblemished life we once enjoyed in the Garden of Eden. While we may one day resume this sublime existence in Heaven, the sins of Adam and Eve have deprived us of that possibility on earth. Beauty, then, is a fragment of the divine, and the sight of it saddens us by evoking our sense of loss and our yearning for the life denied us. The qualities written into beautiful objects are those of a God from whom we live far removed, in a world mired in sin. But works of art are finite enough, and the care taken by those who create them great enough, that they can claim a measure of perfection ordinarily unattainable by human beings. These works are bitter-sweet tokens of a goodness to which we still aspire, however infrequently we may approach it in our actions or our thoughts.

Even stripped of its theological elements, this story helps to account for the sorrow that can cling to our encounters with attractive objects. Imagine a man in an especially tormented period, sitting in the waiting room of a Georgian townhouse before a meeting. Uninterested in the magazines on offer, he looks up at the ceiling and recognises that at some point in the eighteenth century, someone took the trouble to design a complicated but harmonious moulding made up of interlocking garlands of flowers and painted it a mixture of white, porcelain blue and yellow. The ceiling is a repository of the qualities the man would like to have more of in himself: it manages to be both playful and serious, subtle and clear, formal and unpretentious. Though it must have been commissioned by people no less practical than he, it has a profound unsentimental sweetness, like that of a smile breaking across a child's face. At the same time, the man is aware that the ceiling contains everything that he does not. He is embroiled in professional complications which he cannot resolve, he is permanently tired, a sour expression is etched onto his face, and he has begun shouting intemperately at strangers – when all he wants to explain is that he is in pain. The ceiling is the man's true home, to which he cannot find his way back. There are tears in his eyes when an assistant enters the room to usher him to his meeting.

The man's sadness points us to a subsidiary claim. It is perhaps when our lives are at their most problematic that we are likely to be most receptive to beautiful things. Our downhearted moments provide architecture and art with their best openings, for it is at such times that our hunger for their ideal qualities will be at its height. It is not those creatures with well-organised, uncluttered minds who will be most moved by the sight of a clean and empty room in which sunlight washes over a generous expanse of concrete and wood, nor will it be the man with every confidence that his affairs are in order who will crave to live under – and perhaps even shed a tear over – the ceilings of a Robert Adam townhouse.

7.
While a common reaction to seeing a thing of beauty is to want to buy it, our real desire may be not so much to own what we find beautiful as to lay permanent claim to the inner qualities it embodies.

A human ideal on a ceiling.
Robert Adam, Home House, Portman Square, London, 1775

Owning such an object may help us realise our ambition of absorbing the virtues to which it alludes, but we ought not to presume that those virtues will automatically or effortlessly begin to rub off on us through tenure. Endeavouring to purchase something we think beautiful may in fact be the most unimaginative way of dealing with the longing it excites in us, just as trying to sleep with someone may be the bluntest response to a feeling of love.

What we seek, at the deepest level, is inwardly to resemble, rather than physically to possess, the objects and places that touch us through their beauty.

1.

An antique shop on one of north-west London's more ragged edges. Outside, ambulance sirens hint at the homicidal conclusions to disagreements, police helicopters hover overhead, and people with unmatched socks advance down the street announcing millennial disasters to indifferent passers-by.

But the term 'antique shop' may be too quaint and tactful to capture the nature of this establishment. There are no smells of old leather and salesmen with half-moon glasses here; this more closely resembles a bailiff's depot or junk yard. This is where objects make a last attempt to tempt the partially sighted before they are carted off to erode in a landfill.

In one corner stands an especially grievous-looking item, a sideboard with bulbous wings, two bay windows, Corinthian columns and a gilt-edged mirror. Though the piece's drawers still work and the finish remains miraculously unspoilt, its price is closer to that of firewood than furniture, testifying to an ugliness too blatant for even the most generous-minded or myopic to ignore.

And yet how loved this sideboard must once have been. A maid might have run her duster over it every few days in an ample house in Richmond or Wimbledon. A cat perhaps playfully rubbed its tail against it on the way into the living room. For a generation, it would have proudly displayed Christmas pudding, champagne glasses and wedges of Stilton. But now, in the corner of this shop, it has all the poignancy of an ageing exiled Russian princess, dreaming of a palace in St Petersburg from a fleapit in Paris, letting all who will listen know of how attractive she looked at seventeen – even as despair and alcohol hang heavy on her breath.

Finding things beautiful naturally invites us to imagine that we will remain loyal to our feelings. But the histories of design and architecture offer little reassurance as to the fidelity of our tastes. The fate of the side-board imitates that of numberless mansions, concert halls and chairs. Our impressions of beauty continually swing between stylistic polarities: between the restrained and the exuberant; the rustic and the urban; the feminine and the masculine – leading us ruthlessly to abandon objects to expire in junk shops at every swerve.

Precedent forces us to suppose that later generations will one day walk around our houses with the same attitude of horror and amusement with which we now consider many of the possessions of the dead. They will marvel at our wallpapers and our sofas and laugh at aesthetic crimes to which we are impervious. This awareness can lend to our affections a fragile, nervous quality. Knowing that what we now love may in the future, for reasons beyond our current understanding, appear absurd is as hard to bear in the context of a piece of furniture in a shop as it is in the context of a prospective spouse at an altar.

No wonder, then, that architects so assiduously try to distinguish their craft from fashion, and that they set such store (in vain, of course) on creating works which the decades will not render ridiculous.

2.

Why do we change our minds about what we find beautiful?

In 1907 a young German art historian named Wilhelm Worringer published an essay entitled 'Abstraction and Empathy', in which he attempted to explain our shifts from a psychological perspective.

He began by suggesting that during the span of human history there had been only two basic types of art, 'abstract' and 'realistic', either one of which might, at any given time in a particular society, be favoured over the other. Through the millennia, the abstract had enjoyed popularity in Byzantium, Persia, Papua New Guinea, the Solomon Islands, Congo, Mali and Zaire, and it was just then, at the opening of the twentieth century, returning to prominence in the West. This was an art governed by a spirit of symmetry, order, regularity and geometry. Whether in the form of sculpture or carpets, mosaics or pottery, whether in the work of a basket weaver from Wewak or that of a painter from New York, abstract art aspired to create a tranquil atmosphere marked by flat, repetitive visual planes, the whole being free of any allusion to the living world.

By contrast, Worringer noted, realistic art, which had dominated aesthetics in the Ancient Greek and Roman eras and held sway in Europe from the Renaissance to the late nineteenth century, sought to evoke the vibrancy and colour of tangible experience. Artists of this stripe strove to capture the atmosphere of a threatening pine forest, the texture of human blood, the swelling of a teardrop or the ferocity of a lion.

The most compelling aspect of Worringer's theory – a point as readily applicable to architecture as it is to painting – was his explanation of why a society might transfer its loyalty from the one aesthetic mode to the other. The determinant lay, he believed, in those values which the society in question was lacking, for it would love in art whatever it did not possess in sufficient supply within itself. Abstract art, infused as it was with harmony, stillness and rhythm, would appeal chiefly to societies yearning for calm – societies in which law and order were fraying, ideologies were shifting, and a sense of physical danger was compounded by moral and spiritual confusion. Against such a turbulent background (the sort of atmosphere to be found in many of the metropolises of twentieth-century America or in New Guinean villages enervated by generations of internecine strife), inhabitants would experience what Worringer termed 'an immense need for tranquillity', and so would turn to the abstract, to patterned baskets or the minimalist galleries of Lower Manhattan.

But in societies which had achieved high standards of internal and external order, so that life therein had come to seem predictable and overly secure, an opposing hunger would emerge: citizens would long

We respect a style which can move us away from what we fear and towards what we crave:
Top left: raffia skirt, Kuba, twentieth century
Top right: Agnes Martin, *Untitled*, 1962
Bottom: Byzantine mosaic, Basilica of Kampanopetra, Cyprus, sixth century AD

to escape from the suffocating grasp of routine and predictability – and would turn to realistic art to quench their psychic thirst and reacquaint themselves with an elusive intensity of feeling.

We can conclude from this that we are drawn to call something beautiful whenever we detect that it contains in a concentrated form those qualities in which we personally, or our societies more generally, are deficient. We respect a style which can move us away from what we fear and towards what we crave: a style which carries the correct dosage of our missing virtues. That we need art in the first place is a sign that we stand in almost permanent danger of imbalance, of failing to regulate our extremes, of losing our grip on the golden mean between life's great opposites: boredom and excitement, reason and imagination, simplicity and complexity, safety and danger, austerity and luxury.

If the behaviour of babies and small children is any guide, we emerge into the world with our tendencies to imbalance already well entrenched. In our playpens and high chairs, we are rarely far from displaying either hysterical happiness or savage disappointment, love or rage, mania or exhaustion – and, despite the growth of a more temperate exterior in adulthood, we seldom succeed in laying claim to lasting equilibrium, traversing our lives like stubbornly listing ships on choppy seas.

Our innate imbalances are further aggravated by practical demands. Our jobs make relentless calls on a narrow band of our faculties, reducing our chances of achieving rounded personalities and leaving us to suspect (often in the gathering darkness of a Sunday evening) that much of who we are, or could be, has gone unexplored. Society ends up containing a range of unbalanced groups, each hungering to sate its particular psychological deficiency, forming the backdrop against which our frequently heated conflicts about what is beautiful play themselves out.

A wall to defend us against the threat of poverty and degradation:
Top: bedroom of Mme Adélaïde, Palace of Versailles, 1765
A defence against the dangers of privilege:
Bottom: Tomas Nollet and Hilde Huyghe, Nollet and Huyghe House, Bruges, 2002

3.

Viewed in this light, a given stylistic choice will tell us as much about what its advocates lack as about what they like. We can understand a seventeenth-century elite's taste for gilded walls by simultaneously remembering the context in which this form of decoration developed its appeal: one where violence and disease were constant threats, even for the wealthy – fertile soil from which to begin appreciating the corrective promises offered by angels holding aloft garlands of flowers and ribbons.

We shouldn't believe that the modern age, which often prides itself on rejecting signs of gentility and leaves walls unplastered and bare, is any less deficient. It is merely lacking different things. An absence of politesse is no longer the prevailing dread. In most Western cities, at least, the worst of the slums have been replaced by clean, well-charted streets. Life in much of the developed world has become rule-bound and materially abundant, punctilious and routine, to the extent that longings now run in another direction: towards the natural and unfussy, the rough and authentic – longings that bourgeois households may rely on unrendered walls and breeze blocks to help them to assuage.

4.

Historians have often noted that the Western world in the late eighteenth century acquired a taste for the natural in all its major art forms. There was new enthusiasm for informal clothing, pastoral poetry, novels about ordinary people and unadorned architecture and interior decoration. But we shouldn't be led by this aesthetic shift to conclude that the inhabitants of the West were at this time becoming any more natural in themselves. They were falling in love with the natural in their art precisely because they were losing touch with the natural in their own lives.

Thanks to advances in technology and trade, existence for the European upper classes had become, by this period, overly safe and procedural, an excess which the educated looked to relieve through holidays in cottages and readings of couplets on flowers. In his essay 'On Naive and Sentimental Poetry' (1796), Friedrich Schiller observed that the Ancient Greeks, who had spent most of their time outdoors, whose cities were small and ringed by forests and seas, had only rarely felt the need to celebrate the natural world in their art. 'Since the Greeks had not lost nature in themselves,' he explained, 'they had no great desire to create objects external to them in which they could recover it.' And then, turning to his own day, Schiller drove home his message: 'However, as nature begins gradually to vanish from human life as a direct experience, so we see it emerge in the world of the poet as an idea. We can expect that the nation which has gone the farthest towards unnaturalness would have to be touched most strongly by the phenomenon of the naive. This nation is France' – a country whose late queen had only a few years before perfectly corroborated Schiller's thesis by passing her weekends watching cows being milked in the rustic village she had had built at the end of her garden.

5.

In 1776 the Swiss artist Caspar Wolf painted a picture of a group of climbers resting in front of the giant Lauteraar glacier high in Switzerland's Bernese Alps. Perched on top of a rock, two of the climbers gaze up at an immense crevasse-pitted floe of ice before them. Their stockings, the shapes of their hats and their expensive-looking and dainty umbrella suggest that they are aristocrats. Below them, at the bottom left of the canvas, oblivious to the view, is a mountain guide, holding a long walking pole and wearing a coarse cloak and a peasant's hat. The painting is a case study in how differing psychological imbalances may result in contrasting notions of beauty.

Though he must know these mountains better than all his charges, the guide has none of the aristocrats' interest in the scene. He seems to be

Cottages to correct the excesses of a palace:
Marie Antoinette, Prince de Ligne, Hubert Robert,
Queen's Hamlet, Petit Trianon, Versailles, 1785

Caspar Wolf, *The Lauteraar Glacier*, 1776

hiding by the side of a boulder. One imagines him longing for the excursion to be over and inwardly mocking the gentlemen who knocked at his door the previous day, asking to be led into the clouds for lunch, in exchange for a sum he could not turn down. For the guide, beauty is likely to lie in the lowlands, in meadows and chalets, while high mountains are fearsome places which one would sanely ascend only out of necessity, to rescue an animal or to build a snow barrier to break the fury of avalanches.

The date of the picture is significant, for it was at this point in the calendar of the Western imagination that mountains, having been dismissed for centuries as monstrous aberrations, began to exert a widespread attraction for aristocratic tourists, who found in their raw appearance and perilousness a welcome relief from the fastidiousness and gentility of their increasingly over-civilised lives at home. A century before and the gentlemen would have stayed on their estates, trimming their hedges in geometric patterns, feeling no call to be reminded of disorder or wilderness. A century later and even the native guide and his ilk would have started to look more benevolently upon the untamed aspects of nature, their newfound interest having been incubated by the spread of central heating, weather forecasts, newspapers, post offices and railway lines running along even the highest of the Alpine valleys.

But at this moment, at the top of a mountain, two assessments of beauty lie side by side, their divergence explained by two different, and differently deficient, ways of life.

6.

In 1923 a French industrialist named Henry Frugès commissioned the famous but still relatively untried architect Le Corbusier, then thirty-six years old, to build houses for a group of his manual workers and their families. Sited next to Frugès's factories in Lège and Pessac, near

Bordeaux, the resulting complexes were exemplars of Modernism, each a series of undecorated boxes with long rectangular windows, flat roofs and bare walls. Le Corbusier was especially proud of their lack of local and rural allusions. He mocked the aspirations of what he called the 'folkloric brigade' – made up of the sentimentalising traditionalists – and denounced French society's intransigent resistance to modernity. In the houses he designed for the labourers, his admiration for industry and technology expressed itself in expanses of concrete, undecorated surfaces and naked light bulbs.

But the new tenants had a very different idea of beauty. It was not they who had had their fill of tradition and luxury, of gentleness and refinement, nor they who were bored by the regional idiom or the detailed carvings of older buildings. In concrete hangars, dressed in regulation blue overalls, they spent their days assembling pine packing cases for the sugar business. The hours were long and the holidays few. Many had been dragooned from outlying villages to work in Monsieur Frugès's factories, and they were nostalgic for their former homes and parcels of land. At the end of a shift in the plant, to be further reminded of the dynamism of modern industry was not a pressing psychological priority. Within a few years the workers therefore transformed their all-but-identical Corbusian cubes into uniquely differentiated, private spaces capable of reminding them of the things which their working lives had stripped away. Unconcerned with spoiling the great architect's designs, they added to their houses pitched roofs, shutters, small casement windows, flowered wallpaper and picket fences in the vernacular style, and, once that was done, set about installing a variety of ornamental fountains and gnomes in their front gardens.

The tenants' tastes might have run in different directions from those of their architect, but the logic behind the exercise of these tastes was

Le Corbusier, houses, Pessac, 1925 and 1995

identical. Just like the renowned Modernist, the factory workers had fallen for a style evoking the qualities with which their own lives had been insufficiently endowed.

7.

A grasp of the psychological mechanism behind taste may not change our sense of what we find beautiful, but it can prevent us from reacting to what we don't like with simple disbelief. We should know to ask at once what people would have to lack in order to see an object as beautiful and can come to understand the tenor of their deprivation even if we cannot muster enthusiasm for their choice.

We can imagine that a whitewashed rational loft, which seems to us punishingly ordered, might be home to someone unusually oppressed by intimations of anarchy. We can likewise guess that the inhabitants of a roughly rendered building, where the walls are made of black bricks and the doors of rusted steel, are liable to be fleeing from feelings of their own or their society's excessive privilege, just as we can presume that blatantly playful blocks, where the roofs are curved, the windows buckled and the walls painted in childlike colours, will touch an especially powerful chord in the bureaucratic and unimaginative, who will see in them an exuberance that promises an escape from overpowering feelings of inner seriousness.

Our understanding of the psychology of taste can in turn help us to escape from the two great dogmas of aesthetics: the view that there is only one acceptable visual style or (even more implausibly) that all styles are equally valid. A diversity of styles is a natural consequence of the manifold nature of our inner needs. It is only logical that we should be drawn to styles that speak of excitement as well as calm, of grandeur as well as cosiness, given that these are key polarities around which our own lives revolve. As Stendhal knew, 'There are as many styles of beauty as there are visions of happiness.'

The buildings we call beautiful contain in a concentrated form those qualities in which we are deficient:
Left: David Adjaye, Dirty House, London, 2002
Right: Michele Saee and Bruno Pingeot, Publicis Drugstore, Paris, 2004

Nevertheless, this breadth of choice leaves us free to determine that particular works of architecture are more or less adequate responses to our genuine psychological needs. We can accept the legitimacy of the rustic style, even if we question the way M. Frugès's tenants attempted to inject it into their homes at Lège and Pessac. We can condemn the gnomes while respecting the longings which inspired them.

8.

The clashes and evolutions in our sense of what is beautiful may be painful and costly, but there seems little chance of insulating ourselves from them entirely: of producing chairs or sideboards, for instance, which could be guaranteed to provoke a unanimous or permanent aura of charm. Clashes of taste are an inevitable by-product of a world where forces continually fragment and deplete us in new ways. As long as societies and individuals have a history, that is, a record of changing struggles and ambitions, then art, too, will have a history – within which there will always be casualties in the form of unloved sofas, houses and monuments. As the ways in which we are unbalanced alters, so our attention will continue to be drawn to new parts of the spectrum of taste, to new styles which we will declare beautiful on the basis that they embody in a concentrated form what now lies in shadow within us.

1.

When we aren't aiming to be either precise or conclusive, it can be easy
to agree on what a beautiful man-made place might look like. Attempts
to name the world's most attractive cities tend to settle on some familiar
locations: Edinburgh, Paris, Rome, San Francisco. A case will occasionally
be made for Siena or Sydney. Someone may bring up St Petersburg or
Salamanca. Further evidence of our congruent tastes can be found in the
patterns of our holiday migrations. Few people opt to spend the summer
in Milton Keynes or Frankfurt.

Nevertheless, our intuitions about attractive architecture have always
proved of negligible use in generating satisfactory laws of beauty. We
might expect that it would, by now, have grown as easy to reproduce a
city with the appeal of Bath as it is to manufacture consistent quantities
of blueberry jam. If humans were at some point adept at creating a mas-
terwork of urban design, it should have come within the grasp of all suc-
ceeding generations to contrive an equally successful environment at will.
There ought to be no need to pay homage to a city as to a rare creature;
its virtues should be readily fitted to the development of any new piece of
meadow or scrubland. There should be no need to focus our energies on
preservation and restoration, disciplines which thrive on our fears of our
own ineptitude. We should not have to feel alarmed by the waters that lap
threateningly against Venice's shoreline. We should have the confidence
to surrender the aristocratic palaces to the sea, knowing that we could at
any point create new edifices that would rival the old stones in beauty.

Yet architecture has repeatedly defied attempts for it to be set on a more
scientific, rule-laden path. Just as the secrets of good literature have not
been for ever unlocked by the existence of *Hamlet* or *Mansfield Park*, so the
works of Otto Wagner or Sigurd Lewerentz have done nothing to reduce
the proliferation of inferior buildings. The masterpieces of art continue
to seem like chance occurrences and artists to resemble cavemen who

succeed in periodically igniting a flame, without being able to fathom how they did so, let alone communicate the basis of their achievements to others. Artistic talent is like a brilliant firework which streaks across a pitch-black night, inspiring awe among onlookers but extinguishing itself in seconds, leaving behind only darkness and longing.

Even those who privately harbour a notion of the operative principles behind architectural beauty are unlikely to make their suppositions public, for fear of committing an illogicality or of being attacked by the guardians of relativism, who stand ready to censure all those who would dress up individual tastes as objective laws.

2.

Fear has not always been so prevalent. In previous periods, architectural theorists held fervently to the claim that great buildings could be made to yield up their secrets. Architecture was thought as susceptible to rational analysis as any other human or natural phenomenon. The careful study of the finest buildings promised to lead to laws of beauty, whose crisp expression would inspire apprentices, rightfully intimidate clients and spread sympathetic architecture more widely across the earth.

It was in the Renaissance that this sporadic codifying ambition reached an apogee with the publication of Andrea Palladio's *The Four Books of Architecture* (1570), perhaps the West's most influential attempt systematically to decorticate the secrets of successful buildings.

Palladio specified that when designing Ionic columns, a pleasing result could be achieved only if the architrave, frieze and cornice were designed to be one fifth of the height of the column, while a Corinthian capital had to be equal in height to the breadth of the column at its lowest point. With regard to the interior, he insisted that rooms should be at least as high as they were broad, that the correct ratios between the lengths and the sides of rooms were 1:1, 2:3, 3:4 and that a hall should be placed on a central axis, in absolute symmetry to both wings of a house.

3.

Yet, despite the confidence of such assertions, Palladio's laws were not to prove as enduring as the reputations of his houses. What discredited these laws – and indeed spelt the gradual end of any attempt to develop a science of attractive buildings – was the number of exceptions which they seemed to let through with all the regularity of a torn fishing net.

At the northern end of London's Regent's Park stands a mansion, constructed over 400 years after Palladio's treatise was first published, which dutifully follows many of its tenets about proportion, the positioning of rooms, the axes of corridors and the diameters of columns. We might

What laws allow: Quinlan Terry and Raymond Erith, Ionic Villa, London, 1990

expect the house to have been recognised as one of the superlative buildings of contemporary London, an Anglo-Saxon heir to the Villa Rotonda, and yet, in reality, the structure has garnered less flattering verdicts and, among the more forthright, outright ridicule.

The villa's problems are multiple. Its forms seem out of sympathy with their era, they communicate feelings of aristocratic pride which sit oddly with contemporary ideals, the walls are too creamy in colour, while the materials have a lustre and flawlessness that mar the impression of aged dignity which endows Palladio's own villas with charm. One regrets that Palladio found no opportunity to include another two dozen laws of beauty which might have placed additional tourniquets around the many sources of the mansion's failings.

Just as following Palladio seems not to lead us ineluctably towards beauty, so ignoring his advice far from condemns a house to ugliness. Imagine a cottage in the Lake District: its hall is crammed into one corner, its rooms are on no axes at all, its columns are made of thick, untreated oak, its ceilings are hardly the height of a man, and its proportions seem to hew to no mathematical formula whatsoever. And yet such a cottage may profoundly seduce us despite its violation of almost every principle contained in the authoritative pages of *The Four Books of Architecture*.

4.

Such omissions have struck architects hard. In frustration, they have turned against the very idea of laws, declaring them naive and absurd, symptoms of utopian and rigid minds. The concept of beauty has been deemed inherently elusive and therefore quietly sidestepped.

Yet a fairer response to the setbacks associated with Neo-Palladian principles would be greater subtlety rather than nervous silence. Even without knowing the sum of what contributes to the beauty of a building, we should find it possible to venture theories on the subject in the hope of provoking others to contribute further and complementary ideas to an evolving body of knowledge.

To help overcome our reluctance to pass open judgement on the aesthetic side of buildings, we should consider our comparative confidence in discussing the strengths and failings of our fellow human beings. Much of social conversation amounts to a survey of the different ways in which absent third parties have departed from or, much less commonly, have matched an implicit ideal of behaviour. In both casual and erudite registers, we are drawn to identifying vices and virtues, 'gossip' being only a vernacular version of ethical philosophy. Even though we seldom distil our grudges and admirations into abstract hypotheses, we frequently follow in the footsteps of philosophers who have written treatises aiming to identify and dissect human goodness.

We might learn to put names to the virtues of buildings as these philosophers have done to those of people, carefully pinning down the architectural equivalents of generosity or modesty, honesty or gentleness. Analogising architecture with ethics helps us to discern that there is unlikely ever to be a single source of beauty in a building, just as no one quality can ever underpin excellence in a person. Traits need to arise at congruous moments, and in particular combinations, to be effective. A building of the right proportions which is assembled out of inappropriate materials will be no less compromised than a courageous man lacking in patience or insight.

Armed with a comprehensive list of aesthetic virtues, architects and their clients would be freed from over-reliance on Romantic myths concerning the chance or divine origins of beauty. With virtues better defined and more readily integrated into architectural discussions, we would stand a fairer chance of systematically understanding and re-creating the environments we intuitively love.

Order

1.

From a traffic island at the upper end of a wide Parisian street, the view takes in a symmetrical, spacious corridor of stately apartment buildings, which culminate in a wide square in which a man stands proudly on top of a column. Despite the discord of the world, these blocks have settled their differences and humbly arranged themselves in perfect repetitive patterns, each one ensuring that its roof, façade and materials exactly match those of its neighbours. As far as the eye can see, not a single mansard or railing is out of line. The height of every floor and the position of every window are echoed along and across the street. Arcades rise to balconies which give way to three storeys of weathered sandstone, which in turn meet gently domed, lead-covered roofs, interrupted every few metres by solemn, geometric chimney stacks. The buildings seem to have shuffled forward like a troupe of ballet dancers, each one aligning its toes to the very same point on the pavement as though in obedience to the baton of a strict dancing-master. The dominant rhythm of the blocks is accompanied by subsidiary harmonic progressions, made up of lamps and benches. To the visitor or responsive inhabitant, this spectacle of precision presents an impression of beauty tied to qualities of regularity and uniformity, inviting the conclusion that at the heart of a certain kind of architectural greatness there lies the concept of order.

The street is the product of a distinctively human intelligence. We sense the sheer improbability of nature ever creating anything that could rival this setting for coherence and linearity. The scene confronts us with an externalisation of the most rational, deliberate workings of our minds. We can imagine the tumult that would have preceded the calm which now reigns in this place: the stifling summer days that would have echoed to the hammering and sawing of hundreds of labourers. The materials that make up the street would have had to be gathered from across the country over a period of years by a legion of suppliers, many unaware of their colleagues, all of them working under the guidance of the same master planner. Groups of stonemasons in quarries to the east and south would have spent months striking their chisels in similar configurations, so as to produce stones that would settle uncomplainingly beside their neighbours.

The street speaks of the sacrifice demanded by all works of architecture. The stones might have preferred to continue sleeping where they had lain down to rest at their geological bedtime 200 million years before,

just as the iron ore of the balustrades might have opted to remain lodged in the Massif Central under forests of pine trees, before they were coaxed from their somnolence along with a symphony of other raw materials in order to partake in a colossal urban composition. An artisan's cart would have travelled for days to reach the city, the driver having left behind a family and stayed in cheap inns, so that one day a piece of piping could quietly be united on the second floor of an apartment block with a hand basin, rendering life undramatically but significantly more habitable.

The Parisian street moves us because we recognise how sharply its qualities contrast with those which generally colour our lives. We call it

Charles Percier and Pierre Fontaine, rue de Castiglione, Paris, 1802

beautiful from a humbling overfamiliarity with its antitheses: in domestic life, with sulks and petty disputes, and in architecture, with streets whose elements crossly decide to pay no heed to the appearance of their neighbours and instead cry out chaotically for attention, like jealous and enraged lovers. This ordered street offers a lesson in the benefits of surrendering individual freedom for the sake of a higher and collective scheme, in which all parts become something greater by contributing to the whole. Though we are creatures inclined to squabble, kill, steal and lie, the street reminds us that we can occasionally master our baser impulses and turn a waste land, where for centuries wolves howled, into a monument of civilisation.

2.

Order contributes to the appeal of almost all substantial works of architecture. So fundamental is this quality, in fact, that it is written into even the most modest of projects at their very inception, in careful diagrams of electricity circuits and pipework, in elevations and plans – documents of beauty in which every cable and door frame has been measured and in which, though we may fail to grasp the exact meaning of certain symbols and numbers, we may nonetheless sense, and delight in, the overwhelming presence of precision and intent.

'You like to complain that these dry numbers are the opposite of poetry!' scolded Le Corbusier, frustrated that we might overlook the beauty inherent in such plans and in the forms of symmetrical bridges, blocks and squares. 'These things are beautiful because in the middle of the apparent incoherence of nature or the cities of men, they are places of geometry, a realm where practical mathematics reigns... And is not geometry pure joy?'

Joy because geometry represents a victory over nature and because, despite what a sentimental reading might suggest, nature is in truth

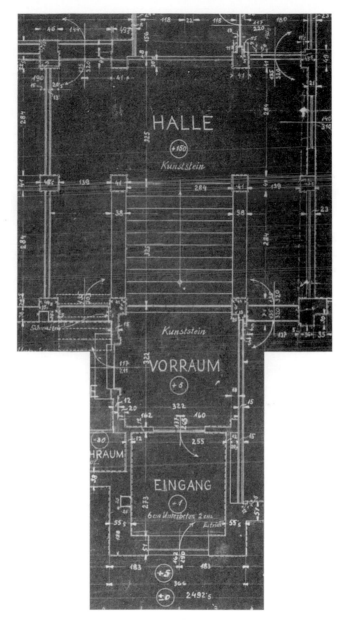

The pure joy of geometry:
Ludwig Wittgenstein, plan, Wittgenstein House, Vienna, 1928

opposed to the order we rely on to survive. Left to its own devices, nature will not hesitate to crumble our roads, claw down our buildings, push wild vines through our walls and return every other feature of our carefully plotted geometric world to primal chaos. Nature's way is to corrode, melt, soften, stain and chew on the works of man. And eventually it will win. Eventually we will find ourselves too worn out to resist its destructive centrifugal forces: we will grow weary of repairing roofs and balconies, we will long for sleep, the lights will dim, and the weeds will be left to spread their cancerous tentacles unchecked over our libraries and shops. Our background awareness of inevitable calamity is what can make us especially sensitive to the beauty of a street, in which we recognise the very qualities on which our survival hangs. The drive towards order reveals itself as synonymous with the drive towards life.

3.

Architectural order attracts us, too, as a defence against feelings of over-complication. We welcome man-made environments which grant us an impression of regularity and predictability, on which we can rely to rest our minds. We don't, in the end, much like perpetual surprises.

A sign of just how little we appreciate them is the lengths to which we often go to take in a view. We delight in reaching hill-tops, panoramic terraces, skyline restaurants and observation posts, where we encounter the basic pleasure of being able to see what lies in the far distance, and can follow roads and rivers across the landscape, rather than have them surge ahead of us without notice.

A comparable pleasure can be found in buildings, for example at the window of a country house which gives out onto a long regular driveway, or in a corridor extending from one extremity of a house to the other, or in a series of courtyards on a perfect axis. In these manifestations of ordered construction, we are granted a feeling of having tamed the unpredictabilities

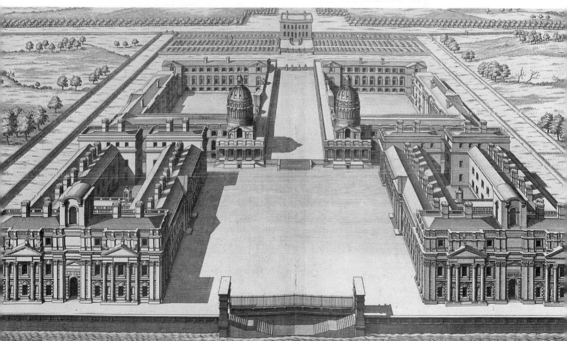

The pleasures of an ordered view:
Top: Carl Frederik Adelcrantz, Sturehof Estate, near Stockholm, 1781
Bottom: Christopher Wren and his successors, Greenwich Hospital, *c.* 1695

to which we are subject and, in a symbolic way, acquired command over a disturbingly unknowable future.

4.

Though we tend to believe, in architecture as in literature, that an important work should be complicated, many appealing buildings are surprisingly simple, even repetitive in their designs. The beguiling terraced houses of Bloomsbury or the apartment buildings of central Paris are assembled according to an unvarying and singularly basic pattern, once laid down in forceful municipal building codes. Over generations, these codes prevented architects from using their imaginations; they handcuffed them to a narrow palette of acceptable materials and forms, and, like the institution of marriage, restricted choice in the name of delivering the satisfactions of restraint.

That building codes have disappeared in many cities, and the modest ordered but satisfying edifices along with them, can be traced back to a perverse dogma which overtook the architectural profession in the Romantic period: a faith in a necessary connection between architectural greatness and originality. Over the nineteenth century, architects came to be rewarded according to the uniqueness of their work, so that constructing a new house or office in a familiar form grew no less contemptible than plagiarising a novel or poem.

This emphasis on individual genius had the unintended effect of tearing apart the carefully woven fabric of cities. 'A day never passes without our hearing our architects called upon to be *original* and to invent a new style,' observed John Ruskin in 1849, bewildered by the sudden loss of visual harmony. What could be more harmful, he asked, than to believe that a 'new architecture is to be invented fresh every time we build a workhouse or parish church?' He proposed that architecture should be the work of '*one* school, so that from the cottage to the palace, and from the chapel to the basilica, every feature of the architecture of the nation shall be as commonly current as its language or its coin'. Half a century later and in a similar vein, Adolf Loos appealed to architects to put aside their individual ambitions for the sake of collective coherence: 'The best form is there already and no one should be afraid of using it, even if the basic idea for it comes from someone else. Enough of our geniuses and their originality. Let us keep on repeating ourselves. Let one building be like another. We won't be published in *Deutsche Kunst und Dekoration* and we won't be made professors of applied art, but we will have served ourselves, our times, our nation and mankind to the best of our ability.'

Few architects have listened. A commission for a house or an office remains an opportunity to reconsider from first principles the design of a window frame or front door. But an architect intent on being different may in the end prove as troubling as an over-imaginative pilot or doctor. However important originality may be in some fields, restraint and adherence to procedure emerge as the more significant virtues in a great many others. We rarely wish to be surprised by novelty as we round street corners. We require consistency in our buildings, for we are ourselves frequently close to disorientation and frenzy. We need the discipline offered by similarity, as children need regular bedtimes and familiar, bland foods. We require that our environments act as guardians of a calmness and direction on which we have a precarious hold. The architects who benefit us most may be those generous enough to lay aside their claims to genius in order to devote themselves to assembling graceful but predominantly unoriginal boxes. Architecture should have the confidence and the kindness to be a little boring.

5.

Then again, our love of order is not without limit, as we will recognise when we stand in front of a multistorey office building whose every window consists of an identical square of reflective glass locked into an identical aluminium frame, whose every floor resembles every other, which makes no obvious distinctions between right and left or front and back, and on whose surface not even a stray aerial or security camera is allowed to disturb the harmony of a master grid. Rather than exciting our admiration with evidence of its ordered nature, such a box may provoke feelings of lassitude or irritation. In its presence, we are likely to forget the effort that would have been required to wrest order out of chaos – and instead of praising the building for its regularity, we may condemn it for its tedium.

Insofar as we appreciate order, it is when we perceive it as being accompanied by complexity, when we feel that a variety of elements has been brought to order – that windows, doors and other details have been knitted into a scheme that manages to be at once regular and intricate. Thus, in St Mark's Square in Venice, it is the façade of the Doge's Palace

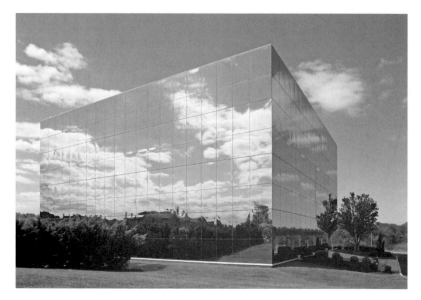

The limits of order:
Office building, Trenton, New Jersey, 1995

which arrests and enchants us, not that of the Procuratie Vecchie, for though both façades are programmatic, only the palace's is endowed with a pattern sufficiently elaborate to render vivid a sense of order. This great Gothic box, in which no one storey duplicates any other in its height or decorative motif, confidently holds our gaze as we try to decipher in its forms an intelligence we can intimate but not immediately understand. There is no simple system of repetition at work here. The top-floor windows and ground-floor arches are of the same family and yet are variously sized and interspaced. The cloverleaf niches at the very top echo the carvings over the columns of the first-floor gallery, without, however, being aligned with them, each storey seeming to pursue a congruent but independent path. There are shifts of mood as the eye ascends the façade, so that whereas the ground floor conveys a sensible and workmanlike air, with feet dug plainly and uncomplainingly into the ground, the first floor takes on the character of an embroidered dress. The smooth mass of white and pink brickwork which sits above evokes a patterned tablecloth, with the arches of the gallery now transformed into tassels and the ground-floor arches into table legs. The whole ends on a joyful note, the decorations of the roof line hinting at carnival hats saluting the skies of Venice.

By comparison, there are no puzzles to detain or astonish us in the Classical front of the Procuratie Vecchie. The eye at once deduces the scheme behind its design, where the ground floor sets a pattern which is unimaginatively imitated on a smaller scale on both the first and second floors. The difference between this building and the Doge's Palace is like the difference between a monotone drum beat and a Bach fugue.

6.

The most obvious means of creating complexity in a façade is through variations in the handling of doors and windows. But a pleasingly complex effect can also be attained through the use of brick, limestone, marble,

The tedium of order: Mauro Coducci, Procuratie Vecchie, Venice, 1532

patinated copper, wood and concrete, materials somewhat rough and uncivilised in appearance, in each of which something organic and untamed seems to stir. Beauty is a likely offspring when order is imposed on such vital materials: when spirit is aligned with logic. As Novalis advised: 'In a work of art, chaos must shimmer through the veil of order.'

There are masonry walls that perfectly honour the German poet's insight, where every brick seems alive, unruly and individual, freighted with a distinctive personality and story. One brick may be gnarled and dark, another pink and innocent, a third stubbornly small, a fourth coloured and textured like walnut bread. Yet all these disparate characters

The pleasure of order combined with complexity: Doge's Palace, Venice, 1340–1420

will settle side by side, end to end, in creamy mortar, conforming to the selfsame master scheme, perfectly balanced between singularity and concord.

Flagstone floors can present us with a similar picture of harmony between contrary forces. There are floors in which large, obtuse stones have been persuaded by a mason to take their place within a methodical grid. One senses how the excesses in the character of these stones was tempered, how they were educated out of the savagery still evident in the craggy cliff-faces from which they were heaved. They had to surrender their defiance, trim their mossy beards, and smooth their warts and

bunions, all for the sake of communal discipline – contributing to a floor where, as we make our way across it, we can appreciate order without danger of boredom and vigour without the shadow of anarchy.

Wooden floors offer analogous pleasures when planks, which once had the pulse of nature flowing through them, submit to the will of the saw and yet when, within each plank, enough signs of life remain to counterpoint the carpenter's geometry. We can see eddies, swirls and imperfections, as if the wood were a turbulent but frozen river. Irregularities remain – a knot that hasn't been planed down, or a dip or buckle that hasn't been smoothed – and yet these features are gracious rather than threatening, reminders of complexity, for they are neatly contained within a series of calm parallel lines and right angles, fixed in formation by long iron nails.

The animating tension between order and chaos can be explored not only through materials but also through contours and sites. John Nash's Park Crescent in Marylebone, for example, had it been laid out in a straight line, would have amounted to a relatively banal row of terraced houses. What advances its particular beauty is our sense that the order it displays has been achieved against the contrary and subversive pull exerted by a curve. We can imagine the difficulty involved in setting each building at a finely graded angle to its neighbours, and in moulding a façade around the recalcitrant arc of a semicircle.

In Diener and Diener's Langhaus apartment block in Amsterdam's eastern docklands, a massive, highly repetitive structure finds its regularity mitigated by the combination of an asymmetrical rhythm in the windows (6:12:21), the coarse, variegated bricks of the façades and the siting of the block on the edge of a sombre, tempestuous waterway – details which ensure that the building will end up on the correct, magnificent side of ordered.

In an adjoining part of the same Dutch development, a strict building code forces rows of terraced houses to adopt identical dimensions, a width of 4.2 metres and a height of 9.5 metres. Yet within these bounda ries, a high degree of exuberance and inventiveness is allowed in terms of materials, window styles and individual floor heights. As our eyes scan the façades fronting the canals, we delight in their variations while admiring the rigorous parameters within which they play themselves out. A similar ethic obtains in Telč, in the Czech Republic, where the rigid ground plan specified for the houses which line the main square is offset by a liberal attitude towards colours, mouldings and roof shapes. The result recalls an endearing line-up of schoolchildren whose chief (and perhaps only) resemblance consists in being all of the same height.

Diener and Diener, Langhaus, Java Island, Amsterdam, 2001

7.

Such works emphasise the truth of the ancient maxim that beauty lies between the extremities of order and complexity. Just as we cannot appreciate the attractions of safety without a background impression of danger, so, too, it is only in a building which flirts with confusion that we can apprehend the scale of our debt to our ordering capacities.

Top left: West 8/Borneo Sporenburg Houses, Amsterdam, 1997
Bottom left: Main Square, Telč, South Moravia, sixteenth century

Flirting with being boring, rescued by the scale and the curve:
John Nash, Park Crescent, 1812

Remove either one, and something is lost:
Karljosef Schattner, Institute of Journalism, Eichstätt, 1987

Balance

1.

Beneath the pleasure generated by the juxtaposition of order and complexity, we can identify the subsidiary architectural virtue of *balance*. Beauty is a likely outcome whenever architects skilfully mediate between any number of oppositions, including the old and the new, the natural and the man-made, the luxurious and the modest, and the masculine and the feminine.

2.

For decades the U-shaped Baroque building which houses the Institute of Journalism in Eichstätt had a courtyard in the middle, empty save for a flower bed and a bicycle rack. Then, in the mid 1980s, pressure for space led the institute's trustees to commission a new structure from the architect Karljosef Schattner, who dropped an unapologetically modern concrete and glass block into the void between the existing gabled and decorated wings. Although dramatically different in style, the old and new parts have nevertheless achieved a seductive harmony as well as a curious codependence, with each relying on the other to downplay its faults and enhance its charms. Removing either building would render the remaining one pedantically hidebound or brutally modern, while together they accomplish a beguiling synthesis of emotional temperaments.

In the lobby of Louis Kahn's Yale Center for British Art, in New Haven, another reconciliation of opposites is effected through the interplay of concrete walls and inset panels made of English oak. It would be hard to name two materials with less in common than this pair. The strength, longevity and nobility of oak have long furnished the English with an idealised image of their own character. It is against backgrounds of richly textured oak that generations of gentlemen have read the *Daily*

Telegraph in their clubs and dons have lunched in Oxbridge colleges. It was in oak trees that Robin Hood escaped the law and Charles II hid from Cromwell's armies. It was English oak that provided Westminster Abbey with its ceiling and Nelson's navy with its ships. Around polished panels of the wood, there therefore hover associations of rural life, aristocracy, history, the smells of leather and whisky – not to mention romantic notions of nationhood.

We are far from all of this with concrete, a material which embodies speed, economy and, in its reinforced variety, brute might. It is a quintessentially modern, democratic medium whose rediscovery by architects in the early twentieth century made possible many of the overtly functional structures of the technological age, including grain silos, garages, tower blocks and warehouses.

However, like an intelligent host faced with a couple of dinner guests from sharply opposed worlds, Kahn helps these two unlike elements to acknowledge each other's virtues and surmount their mutual suspicion. He manages to reconcile them by making no attempt to disguise or minimise their differences. Unembarrassed to leave his concrete bare and unafraid to emphasise its poverty and starkness, Kahn encourages us to discover a new kind of beauty in its elephant-grey massing. At the same time, he lets us openly savour and celebrate the antique pleasures of oak, showing to full advantage the warm tones, clarity and striated grain with which time endowed it. As befits a building dedicated to the paintings of a nation more tortured than most by the competing claims of history and modernity, the Yale Center for British Art delivers an elegant essay on how past and present might learn to coexist and complement each other. In doing so, it sketches for us the dimensions of an ideal contemporary Englishness.

High in the Italian Alps, yet another building resolves a comparable tension between the country and the city, and the agrarian and the industrial. Herzog and de Meuron's Stone House consists of an exposed

An ideal contemporary Englishness: Louis Kahn, Yale Center for British Art, New Haven, 1977

Herzog and de Meuron, Stone House, Tavole, Liguria, 1988

concrete frame within which are set loose, mortarless stones quarried from the surrounding slopes. These stones, of the type used for centuries to build the region's barns and farmhouses, are so irregular in colour and shape as to teeter on the edge of rustic incoherence, to be saved from it only by the rational geometry of their concrete frame. Like Kahn's Yale Center, Herzog and de Meuron's house achieves its effect by weaving a pattern of beauty from two aesthetic strands – meaning, also, two varieties of happiness – which we would never previously have imagined belonging together.

3.
To explain the appeal of balance between contrasting elements in buildings, it seems natural to move the discussion beyond architecture, for it is not only visual beauty which draws us to these balanced works, but also, and perhaps even principally, the evidence they emit of possessing a distinctively human kind of goodness, or maturity.

It appears we cannot keep ourselves from semiconsciously reading our own dynamics into buildings and correlating the oppositions that certain examples display with competing sides of our own characters. The tension between curves and straight lines in a façade carries echoes of the pull between reason and emotion in ourselves. It is a human integrity that we see in unvarnished wood, and a human hedonism in gilded panels. Panes of glass etched with imprints of flowers and black concrete blocks (such as those found on the exterior walls of the University Library in Utrecht) seem the natural twins of masculine and feminine traits.

It follows that the balance we approve of in architecture, and which we anoint with the word 'beautiful', alludes to a state that, on a psychological level, we can describe as mental health or happiness. Like buildings, we, too, contain opposites which can be more or less successfully handled. We, too, can descend towards extremes – of chaos or rigidity, decadence

Men and women: Wiel Arets, University Library, Utrecht, 2004

or austerity, machismo or effeminacy – even as we instinctively recognise that our well-being depends on our being able both to accommodate and to cancel out our polarities.

Our attempts to harmonise our different aspects isn't generally helped by the world around us, which tends to emphasise a range of awkward antitheses. Consider, for instance, the truisms which hold that one cannot be at the same time both funny and serious, democratic and refined, cosmopolitan and rural, practical and elegant, or masculine and delicate.

Balanced buildings beg to differ. Take, for example, the traditional antithesis between luxury and simplicity. The idea of luxury has tended to be associated with grandeur, pomposity and arrogance – while simplicity has been equated variously with squalor, incompetence and inelegance. However, the interior of Skogaholm Manor in Sweden, decorated towards the end of the eighteenth century, triumphantly contradicts any inclination to render the pairing of these two qualities impossible.

The furniture is detailed in a refined Rococo manner, carved with gentle,

A balanced building as a promise of a balanced life:
Interior, Skogaholm Manor, Närke, *c.* 1790

aristocratic curves and garlands of flowers. But as the eye moves towards the ground, something unusual comes into view. Where we might expect the chairs to meet a floor which resembled them in tone – made of marble, perhaps, or highly veneered parquetry – we instead find rough, unvarnished wooden planks, of the sort one might see in a hayloft. A similarly striking combination can be seen in the wall decorations, whose Neoclassical floral motifs, which might more predictably have been coloured in rich reds and golds, are instead executed in muted greys and browns.

The manor house proposes a new human ideal, in which luxury would entail neither decadence nor a loss of contact with the democratic truths of the soul, and in which simplicity could be synthesised with nobility and refinement.

If certain subtly balanced buildings touch us, it is because they stand as exemplars of how we might adjudicate between the conflicting aspects of our characters, how we, too, might aspire to make something beautiful of our troubling opposites.

1.

For the traveller who sets out from Zurich on a summer's morning on a train bound south, for the Alps, the view is initially of a rolling pastoral landscape, in which cows feast on luminously green grass and occasionally glance up at the passing carriages with sad, almost wise brown eyes. For an hour, at least, nature is at her most benevolent. It is only beyond the town of Chur that the bucolic scene gives way to something more severe. The lush grass is gradually replaced by a terrain strewn with rubble and rock. Sheer walls of granite shoot up by the side of the train, alternating with precipitous canyons, silent but for the call of eagles and the cracking of branches. Along implausibly steep mountainsides, families of pine trees cling to narrow ledges like diligent soldiers on watch. While inside the carriage, everything remains as it was in the lowlands – pictures of a lake are still neatly screwed to the wall by the door, a bottle of apple juice continues to sit undrunk on the table – outside, we have journeyed to a place which resembles one of the less hospitable moons of Jupiter.

In a valley so steep that its gelatinous walls seem never to have been warmed by the sun, a drop of hundreds of feet ends in a furious brown river clotted with stones and brambles. As the train curves around the mountainside, a view opens up along its length, revealing that, several carriages ahead, the burgundy-red locomotive has taken the unexpected decision to cross from one side of the valley to the other, a manoeuvre it proceeds to execute without so much as pausing to confer with higher authorities. It makes its way over the gap, and through a small cloud, with the brisk formality one might associate with the most routine of activities, to which prayer and worship would be at once unnecessary and theatrical supplements. What has rendered this supernatural feat possible is a bridge for which nothing in this setting has prepared us – a perfectly massive yet perfectly delicate concrete bridge, marred by not the slightest stain or impurity, which can only have been dropped from the air by the gods, for we cannot imagine that there would be anywhere in this forsaken spot for humans to rest their tools. The bridge seems unimpressed by the razor-sharp stones around it, by the childish moods of the river and the contorted, ugly grimaces of the rock-face. It stands content to reconcile the two sides of the ravine like an impartial judge, modest and willingly literal-minded about its own achievements, ashamed lest it detain our attention or attract our gratitude.

Yet the bridge testifies to how closely a certain kind of beauty is bound up with our admiration for strength, for man-made objects which can withstand the life-destroying forces of heat, cold, gravity or wind. We see beauty in thick slate roofs that challenge hailstones to do their worst, in sea defences that shrug off the waves which batter them, and in bolts, rivets, cables, beams and buttresses. We feel moved by edifices – cathedrals, skyscrapers, hangars, tunnels, pylons – which compensate for our inadequacies, our inability to cross mountains or carry cables between cities. We respond with emotion to creations which transport us across distances we could never walk, which shelter us during storms we could not weather, which pick up signals we could never hear with our own ears and which hang daintily off cliffs from which we would fall instantly to our deaths.

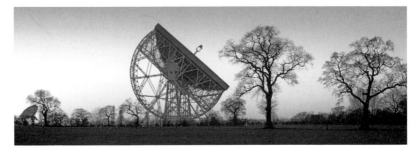

Bernard Lovell, Charles Husband, Lovell Telescope, Jodrell Bank, Cheshire, 1957

2.

It follows from this that the impression of beauty we derive from an architectural work may be proportionally related to the intensity of the forces against which it is pitted. The emotional power of a bridge over a swollen river, for example, is concentrated at the point where the piers meet but resist the waters which rise threateningly around them. We shudder to think of sinking our own feet into such turbulent depths and venerate the bridge's reinforced concrete for the sanguine way it deflects the currents which tyrannise it. Likewise, the heavy stone walls of a lighthouse acquire the character of a forbearing and kindly giant during a spiteful gale which does its best to pant them down, just as in a plane passing through an electrical storm, we can feel something approaching love for the aeronautical engineers who, in quiet offices in Bristol or Toulouse, designed dark grey aluminium wings that could flex through tempests with all the grace of a swan's feathered ones. We feel as safe as we did when we were children being driven home in the early hours by our parents, lying curled up on the backseat under a blanket in our pyjamas, sensing the darkness and cold of the night through the window against which we rested our cheek. There is beauty in that which is stronger than we are.

3.

Nevertheless, because beauty is typically the result of a few qualities working in concert, it can take more to guarantee the appeal of a bridge or a house than strength alone. Both Robert Maillart's Salginatobel and Isambard Brunel's Clifton Suspension bridges are structures of strength; both attract our veneration for carrying us safely across a fatal drop – and yet Maillart's bridge is the more beautiful of the pair for the exceptionally nimble, apparently effortless way in which it carries out its duty. With its ponderous masonry and heavy steel chains, Brunel's construction has something to it of a stocky middle-aged man who hoists his trousers and

Left: Robert Maillart, Salginatobel Bridge, Schiers, 1930
Right: Isambard Brunel, Clifton Suspension Bridge, Bristol, 1864

loudly solicits the attention of others before making a jump between two points, whereas Maillart's bridge resembles a lithe athlete who leaps without ceremony and bows demurely to his audience before leaving the stage. Both bridges accomplish daring feats, but Maillart's possesses the added virtue of making its achievement look effortless – and because we sense it isn't, we wonder at it and admire it all the more. The bridge is endowed with a subcategory of beauty we can refer to as elegance, a quality present whenever a work of architecture succeeds in carrying out an act of resistance – holding, spanning, sheltering – with grace and economy as well as strength; when it has the modesty not to draw attention to the difficulties it has surmounted.

4.

We would not, by this measure, describe a heavy steel beam as elegant if it carried only a tabletop, nor a teacup if its sides were four centimetres thick. Michael Hopkins's canopy for Bracken House is liable to displease us because of the fuss it makes, through multiple bulky struts, of the task of holding up a few relatively light pieces of glass. There is a disproportion between the modest challenge the canopy is set and the laboured response it offers that violates the principles of elegance – just as Santiago Calatrava awes us through the economy and discreet intelligence with which his sculptures defy the pressures of gravity.

In literature, too, we admire prose in which a small and astutely arranged set of words has been constructed to carry a large consignment of ideas. 'We all have strength enough to bear the misfortunes of others,' writes La Rochefoucauld in an aphorism which transports us with an energy and exactitude comparable to that of a Maillart bridge. The Swiss engineer reduces the number of supports just as the French writer compacts into a single line what lesser minds might have taken pages to express. We delight in complexity to which genius has lent an appearance of simplicity.

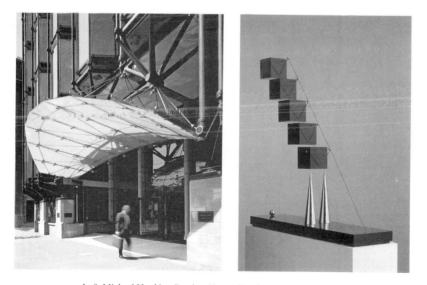

Left: Michael Hopkins, Bracken House, London, 1991
Right: Santiago Calatrava, *Running Torso*, 1985

Left: staircase, Shaker House, Pleasant Hill, Kentucky, 1841
Right: Silvia Gmür and Livio Vacchini, house in Beinweil am See, 1999

5.

For us to deem a work of architecture elegant, it is hence not enough that it look simple: we must feel that the simplicity it displays has been hard won, that it flows from the resolution of a demanding technical or natural predicament. Thus we call the Shaker staircase in Pleasant Hill elegant because we know – without ever having constructed one ourselves – that a staircase is a site complexity, and that combinations of treads, risers and banisters rarely approach the sober intelligibility of the Shakers' work. We deem a modern Swiss house elegant because we note how seamlessly its windows have been joined to their concrete walls, and how neatly the usual clutter of construction has been resolved away. We admire starkly simple works that we intuit would, without immense effort, have appeared very complicated.

6.

Cardinal opportunities for elegance or its opposite lie in the way that columns are designed to hold up ceilings. Even as laypeople, we are adept at guessing the thickness that would be required safely to support a

How we should like to stand in relation to our burdens:
Left: Foster and Partners, Underground Station, Canary Wharf, 1999
Right: The Comares Palace, Alhambra, Granada, 1370

structure and esteem those columns that appear most diffident about the weight they are supporting. Whereas some varieties have broad enough shoulders but look disgruntled at having been asked to carry even a single storey, others hoist up ceilings as high as those of cathedrals without apparent strain, balancing massive weights on their narrow necks as if they were holding aloft a canopy made of linen. We welcome an appearance of lightness, or even daintiness, in the face of downward pressure – columns which seem to offer us a metaphor of how we, too, should like to stand in relation to our burdens.

Windows offer further opportunities for the expression of architectural elegance, the determinant here being the relationship between the amount of glass and the extent of the frame that supports it. When diminutive panes are clasped within heavy, unapologetically broad mountings, we are likely to feel some of the same discomfort as when too many words

A magical ratio of frame to glass, and foot to body:
Left: Marlborough Buildings, Bath, eighteenth century
Right: Edgar Degas, *The Star*, 1879

are being employed to say too little. By contrast, the Georgian houses of Bath charm us by the ethereal way in which the windows appear to hover over their façades. Recognising, as their subsequent colleagues often have not, the intense beauty of the tenderly held pane, the city's eighteenth-century architects competed with each other to develop frames in which the slenderest fingers of wood could fasten around the greatest expanses of glass. Pushing at the technological boundaries, they reduced glazing bars from 38mm (in the earliest houses in Queen Square) to 29mm and eventually to a mere 16 – contributing to windows with some of the same impelling grace as a Degas ballerina, fluidly pirouetting her sylph-like body on an axis of a mere five toes.

7.

If we define elegance as arising in part from the triumph over a given architectural challenge – spanning a river, supporting a ceiling or holding glazing in place – then to the list of challenges we might add the more abstract one of neglect. We appreciate buildings that seem to have shrugged off the weight of carelessness and indifference.

Within the robust arches of Henri Labrouste's Bibliothèque Sainte-Geneviève in Paris, the observant visitor will notice a series of small flowers fashioned out of wrought iron. To think these elegant is to acknowledge how unusual was the care that lay behind their creation. In a busy, often heedless world, they stand as markers of patience and generosity, of a kind of sweetness and even love: a kindness without ulterior motive. They are there for no other reason than that the architect believed they might entertain our eyes and charm our reason. They are markers of politeness, too, the impulse to go beyond what is required to discharge brute tasks – and of sacrifice as well, for it would have been easier to support the iron arches with straight-sided struts. Below, the mood may be workmanlike, and outside, in the streets, there will always be hurry and cruelty, but up

on the ceiling, in a limited realm, flowers swirl and perhaps even laugh as they wend their way around a sequence of arches.

Although we belong to a species which spends an alarming amount of its time blowing things up, every now and then we are moved to add gargoyles or garlands, stars or wreaths, to our buildings for no practical reason whatever. In the finest of these flourishes, we can read signs of goodness in a material register, a form of frozen benevolence. We see in them evidence of those sides of human nature which enable us to thrive rather than simply survive. These elegant touches remind us that we are not exclusively pragmatic or sensible: we are also creatures who, with no possibility of profit or power, occasionally carve friars out of stone and mould angels onto walls. In order not to mock such details, we need a culture confident enough about its pragmatism and aggression that it can also acknowledge the contrary demands of vulnerability and play – a culture, that is, sufficiently unthreatened by weakness and decadence as to allow for visible celebrations of tenderness.

Left: William Kinman (to a design by Robert Adam), detail of
ironwork balusters, 20 St James's Square, London, 1774
Right: friar, Wells Cathedral, Somerset, 1326

1.

For years, on my way to and from the shops, I passed a house which, despite being one of the ugliest buildings I have ever seen, taught me more about architecture than many masterpieces have done.

The house was positioned at one end of a tree-lined avenue in north London, where it attracted my attention through the evidence it gave of having undergone a severe identity crisis. It looked as though each wing and each floor of the house had been designed by a different team of architects, none of which had been permitted any knowledge of the work of its predecessors, so that the collective result was an uncomfortable patchwork of contrasting styles. While some aspects of the house aped the look of a Tudor cottage, others tugged towards the Gothic. There were clashing hints of the vocabularies of the Arts and Crafts movement and the Queen Anne. Even the top floor was contorted, seeming undecided as to whether it wanted to be a mansard or a regular, straight-sided storey.

Signs of an identity crisis: Left: London, NW3
The aesthetics of an English seaside bungalow applied to the dimensions of a skyscraper.
Right: Sidney Kaye, Tower Block, Shepherd's Bush, 1971

2.

A few years later, I moved west, and there began to have similarly strong feelings about a tower block (one of four) on Shepherd's Bush Green, built in the early 1970s by the architect Sidney Kaye. The block was imposing for this part of the capital, twenty storeys high, and visible from as far away as Hampstead. Its height did not, however, prevent it from seeming resolutely squat. Its roof ended dumbly, in a flat plane, below which a series of heavy white bands accentuated the horizontal axis. The windows, meanwhile, made no concession either to their views or to their upward progression, but remained identically shaped and sized from the ground floor to the top. It was as though the aesthetics of a post-war seaside bungalow had been applied to the dimensions of a skyscraper, resulting in a building which was unsure whether it wished to be seen from Hampstead or preferred to nestle modestly amid the dark, low, brick buildings more common to the area. Irritated by its uncertainty, I wanted to demand that it either make itself properly unobtrusive or else make the most of its height and bulk – but, in any case, that it stop straddling the line between meekness and assertion, like an adolescent who insists on taking to the stage but, once there, can only stare mutely and sullenly at the audience.

Not until several years later did I come to understand my dissatisfaction with the tower, thanks to an essay by Louis Sullivan with one of the more intriguing titles in the history of architectural criticism: 'The Tall Office Artistically Considered' (1896). Writing at the dawn of the age of the skyscraper, Sullivan advised his readers that many of the new tall buildings were in danger of stylistic incoherence. The problem was that even as their massing thrust upwards to a height of twenty or thirty storeys, their decorative motifs emphasised the horizontal axis, an orientation better suited to a two-storey Palladian villa. The combination caused them to seem artlessly conflicted about their aims, as if they were

pulling at once upwards and sideways. Sullivan urged architects to let their skyscraper designs be guided by one coherent principle. 'The chief characteristic of the tall building is that it is *lofty*,' he proposed. 'It must be every inch a proud and soaring thing, rising in sheer exultation so that from bottom to top it should be a unit without a single dissenting line.' Within a few years, his suggestion would be consummately realised in the great skyscrapers of New York and Chicago, whose beauty seems the result of just such a decision to speak solely and in unison about height. From their tapered ground-floor entrances to their ruby-red lights blinking at the suburbs from the tips of their radio masts, these tall offices would be everything Sullivan wished: proud, soaring, exultant and inarguably coherent.

3.

When buildings talk, it is never with a single voice. Buildings are choirs rather than soloists; they possess a multiple nature from which arise opportunities for beautiful consonance as well as dissension and discord.

While certain buildings appear to have agreed on their aesthetic mission, persuading their disparate elements to pull together to make a logical contribution to the whole, others seem more conflicted about their intentions, their features heaving querulously in contrary directions. They may disagree about their size, with windows, roofs and doors clashing over questions of precedence. Or their forms may testify to unresolved squabbles about the nature of happiness.

Thus, in the portico of a Viennese villa designed by Otto Wagner, a statue speaks to us of the East, the columns around it of Ancient Greece and the ironwork of rustic Austrian lace, which generates a sense of a chaos nowhere evident in Palladio's Villa Contarini, where the archway

'Every inch a proud and soaring thing':
Cass Gilbert, Woolworth Building, New York, 1913

Left: Otto Wagner, villa, Hüttelbergstrasse 26, Vienna, 1886
Right: Andrea Palladio, Villa Contarini, Padova, 1546

reconciles the columns, the plaster helps to counterpoint the roughness of the stonework and the statue offsets the austerity of the whole.

We could say that nothing in architecture is ever ugly in itself; it is merely in the wrong place or of the wrong size, while beauty is the child of the coherent relationship between parts.

4.

Architectural incoherence is not limited to the designs of individual buildings. It can also, and no less grievously, reside in the relationship between a building and its context, geographical or chronological.

One summer, keen to take a break from routine, I booked myself into the Hotel de l'Europe, a vast red-brick building done up in the Neo-Renaissance style, of a kind often observed in the more expensive districts of Amsterdam. Rooms weren't cheap: a standard double cost ¥42,000 (breakfast was a further ¥2,300 for the simplest order of rice, miso soup and vegetables). But at least the hotel was optimally positioned. It was only a five-minute walk from the Huis Ten Bosch royal palace in The Hague and, in the opposite direction, a ten-minute walk from Utrecht's twelfth-century Nijenrode Castle. There were cheese shops everywhere, teams of Friesian horses and five ancient windmills. Furthermore, a field of 300,000 tulips bordered the buildings, giving way only where the ground began its steep ascent into mountains covered in dense Japanese cedar.

However, none of these details seemed able to shake me from an increasingly peculiar and heavy mood which had settled on me shortly after my arrival at the Hotel de l'Europe. My unhappiness must have had something to do with the fact that, certain appearances to the contrary, I was not in the Netherlands at all but rather in Japan, a forty-minute train ride outside Nagasaki, at a 152-acre theme park named Huis Ten Bosch Dutch Village. This surreal playland had been designed to re-create, with astonishing fidelity, the look of pre-twentieth-century Holland, complete with streets and squares, a network of canals and The Hague's royal palace. In building it, the Japanese, masters of handicraft, had been meticulous in their concern for authenticity: they had consulted original architectural plans and imported wood and bricks from the other side of the world. But such historical exactitude had succeeded only in rendering the place more eerie and unnerving.

The discomfort generated by finding oneself in a corner of the Netherlands in rural Japan alerts us to a further requirement that we might have of buildings: that they should not only harmonise their parts but in addition cohere with their settings; that they should speak to us of the significant values and characteristics of their own locations and eras. For a building to reflect its cultural context may be as central to its mission as that it should respond to its meteorological one – a building which ignores it having the troubling quality of one whose windows fail to open in the tropics or to close in the mountains.

Top: Huis Ten Bosch Dutch Village, Nagasaki, 1992
Bottom: Hotel de l'Europe, Huis Ten Bosch, 1992

5.

Just as it is perturbing when our buildings deny their settings, so it can be pleasurable to find evidence of the opposite tendency – when buildings are marked by distinctly local architectural traits, even of the minor kind that often strike our eyes on touching down in a new country.

A few hours after having arrived in Japan, lying in bed in a Tokyo hotel vainly attempting to sleep, I noticed for the first time just how unusual were the light switches and plugs in my room. The excitement of having arrived in an unknown country coalesced around these fittings, which can be to a building what shoes are to a person: unexpectedly strong indicators of character. I discovered in them harbingers of the national particularities that had motivated my travels. They were promises of a distinctively local kind of happiness. My feelings stemmed not from a naive longing for folkloric exoticism, but from a wish to discover that the genuine differences that exist between lands might find adequate expression on an architectural plane. I wanted light switches, and by extension entire buildings, that could help to signal to me that I was here rather than there and alive now rather than then.

Taking a midnight walk around my hotel, I saw many more signs of an incontrovertibly Japanese identity. In a restaurant, I marvelled at the complex fascia of an electronically controlled toilet. Near a subway station, a vending machine offered bottled water and, as if this were an ordinary snack, packets of dried lobster claws. There were buildings fitted with rows of multicoloured fire-hydrants, and in a supermarket, tubs of seaweed floating in clear jelly. In an arcade, among driving and skiing games, a slot machine challenged me to make arrangements for dinner by catching a weary and confused crab using a set of motor-operated pincers.

I returned to bed and slipped into jet-lagged dreams illuminated by fractured images of neon signs, moss gardens, bullet trains, kimonos and crustaceans.

Marine Catcher, Shinjuku, Tokyo

6.

Unfortunately, the next morning found Tokyo less disposed to indulge my desire for local colour. A practical mood had settled over the city, as twenty million people made their way to work. The streets of the business districts were jammed with cars and dark-suited commuters: I might have been anywhere. With their advertising hoardings unlit, the buildings appeared wilfully ordinary. Clusters of bland skyscrapers dominated the skyline, their pedestrian forms mutely mocking the twelve hours of cloud and snow over which I had flown to reach them. For architectural interest, I might as well have been in Frankfurt or Detroit.

Even in more residential quarters, the architecture was almost entirely lacking in ethnic roots or local flavour. Vast new developments were everywhere, each house assembled of generic materials and forms which would have been unsurprising in almost any part of the developed world. There seemed precious little that was Japanese in Japanese architecture.

The early Modernists would not have complained of this, for they had looked forward to a rational era when local styles would vanish entirely from their profession, as they had done from industrial and product design. There was, after all, no such thing as a local-looking modern bridge or umbrella. Adolf Loos had compared the absurdity of asking for a specifically Austrian kind of architecture to asking for a particularly Austrian-looking bicycle or telephone. If the truth was universal, why demand a local variety of architecture? Tokyo seemed to epitomise the Modernist dream of a place where one might never know from the buildings alone what country one had strayed into.

7.

There were, nevertheless, a few places to turn for aesthetic relief. A friend recommended that I spend a night in an old-fashioned *ryokan,* or inn, faithful in most details to the architecture and design of the Edo period (1615–1868).

Left: skyscrapers, Shiodome, Tokyo
Right: Kamagaya City, Chiba Prefecture, 1993

The *ryokan* was an hour's train ride outside Tokyo, nestled among hills and shrouded in mist. Surrounded by pine trees and a moss garden, it was housed in a long wooden pavilion capped with a traditional *kawarane yane* (tiled roof). A receptionist wearing a kimono and *tabi* (split-toed socks) guided me to my room, which was lined with *fusuma* (sliding doors) and *shoji* (paper) screens decorated with calligraphy. The view was onto a river and a forested slope. Before sunset, I enjoyed an *onsen* (outdoor bath) in an adjacent natural spring, then drank an iced barley tea in an alcove in the garden. Dinner came in a set of immaculate boxes. I savoured the *yose-nabe* (Japanese chowder) and *kounomono* (pickles) – then fell asleep to the sound of water pursuing a path down the mountain side over smooth flat ancient volcanic stones.

But in the morning, my sadness returned at the prospect of having to go back to Tokyo. Disconsolate, I ate a bowl of dried seaweed and ruminated on the schism between the aesthetic perfection of historic Japan and the graceless tedium of its modern incarnation.

On the train journey back, speeding again through a ruined landscape of bland housing estates and apartment blocks, I even began to take exception with the world of the *ryokan*, annoyed at its inability to translate and adapt itself to modern realities, its failure to work out some way to carry over its old charms into a new idiom.

My frustration with the *ryokan* was similar to a feeling I had once experienced in England, on a visit to the traditionally styled village of Poundbury, on the outskirts of Dorchester. Despite its qualified success in capturing the spirit of country life in the eighteenth century, the place was ultimately maddening for its disconnection from the psychological and practical demands of contemporary society. It resembled an ancient relative to whom one was very close as a child, but who lacked any understanding of the adult whom circumstances had in the interim formed, whether for better or worse.

An architecture that cannot accept who we have grown into:
Poundbury, Dorchester, 1994

8.

During my stay, I did see occasional signs that the Japanese were inclined to connect their new buildings with their country's past. But for the most part such attempts seemed half-hearted, overly sentimental or even downright impatient

In a crowded section of Kyoto, atop an innocuous office block, amidst air conditioners and aerials, a tiny traditional shrine looked as if it had been dropped from the air to answer to certain inner needs left unmet by modern architecture. Past and present made no move here towards integration; instead they were happy to coexist, while seeming positive that there was nothing they might do to imbibe each other's strengths.

Elsewhere, apartments had miniature pruned cedar trees outside their entrances and moss gardens in tubs hanging off balconies. I saw

Shijo-dori, Kyoto

calligraphy on shower curtains and *shoji* screens fixed to kitchen doors. I ate in restaurants offering 'authentic ancient rooms' to tourists unbothered by plastic re-creations. The roof of an insurance company or a post office would occasionally curve upwards gently at the edges in a nod to the Tokugawa style.

But the failure of such attempts to rise beyond the kitsch illustrates the difficulties of finding a modern form to embody traditional features of a culture. Paper screens will not necessarily make a house Japanese in spirit; nor will concrete and patinated copper guarantee that it won't be. The true heirs of Tokugawa houses frequently bear no simple outward resemblance to their masters: the resemblance is more subtle, relying on proportions and relations – just as the finest translators of Lady Murasaki are often those who take extensive liberties with individual words, knowing that methodical transposition is rarely the way to stay true to original intentions.

9.

I'd first noted some of the difficulties of translation in a new development in one of London's most famous Classical squares. The architects responsible for the office block which dominates the north-western side of Manchester Square correctly sensed that the handling of the windows was key to harmonising with the existing façades, and so gave their building white rectangular window frames.

Unfortunately, these architects failed to register that Classical frames are noteworthy not because of their colour or shape but because of their slenderness and its associated elegance – qualities which the architects grievously sacrificed by resorting to peculiar and massive frames formed of steel I-beams. Despite their sincere wish to respect the past, the architects had spectacularly bypassed the real reasons why the past might have been worth respecting in the first place. They would have been better off had they taken their guidance from another set of windows entirely, those on the façade of the Queen's Building in Cambridge. Though these frames aren't white but a silvery black, and horizontal rather than vertical, they appear more richly endowed with the true qualities of Classical architecture than any of their counterparts on the apparently more respectful London block. A true homage seldom looks exactly like one.

Left: GMW Architects, north-west side, Manchester Square, London, 2001
Right: south-east side, Manchester Square, late eighteenth century

Classicism in modern guise:
Michael Hopkins, Queen's Building, Emmanuel College, Cambridge, 1995

10.

What, I wondered, might a successful example of modern Japanese architecture look like – one which avoided kitsch and was properly coherent with its place and time?

The national angle to this question has at times, of other countries, been answered in quasi-mystical ways, as if to suggest that borderlines somehow demarcate objective, knowable personalities which the buildings within ought to take a reading of and then passively reflect. In 'On German Architecture' (1772), J. W. Goethe declared that Germany was in its 'essence' a Christian land, and that the only appropriate style for new German buildings was therefore Gothic. On seeing a cathedral, wrote Goethe, 'a German ought to thank God for being able to proclaim aloud, "That is German architecture, our architecture."'

But, in reality, no country ever either owns a style or is locked into it through precedent. National architectural identity, like national identity overall, is created rather than dictated by the soil. History, culture, weather and geography will offer up a great range of possible themes for architects to respond to (not so broad a range as the builders of Huis Ten Bosch may have hoped, perhaps, nor as restricted a one as Goethe proposed). If we end up thinking of certain styles as the indissoluble products of specific places, it is only a tribute to the skill with which architects have coaxed us into seeing the environment through their eyes, and so made their achievements appear inevitable.

At issue, therefore, is not so much what a national style is as what it could be made to be. It is the privilege of architects to be selective about which aspects of the local spirit they want to throw into relief. While most societies experience varying degrees of violence and chaos, for example, we are unlikely to want our buildings to reflect those features of the zeitgeist. Then again, we would feel uncomfortable if architects abandoned reality altogether to produce designs which alluded to none of our prevailing morals or goals. We no more favour delusion in our built environment than we do in individuals.

An adequately contextual building might thus be defined as one which embodies some of the most desirable values and the highest ambitions of its era and place – a building which serves as a repository for a workable ideal.

The attributes of such a building might be compared with those of a prototypically admirable human being in an identical context. Oscar Niemeyer once expressed the wish that his architectural works should share the outlook and attitudes of the most enlightened Brazilians of the era: they should appreciate the burdens and privileges of their country's colonial past without being overwhelmed by them, should be sympathetic to modern technology, yet should retain a healthy playfulness and sensuality. And, above all, he noted, they should indicate their affinity for Brazil's 'white beaches, its huge mountains – and its beautiful tanned women'.

A similar portrait, this time of an ideal Sri Lankan, animates Geoffrey Bawa's Parliament Island on the outskirts of Colombo. Here the buildings

*A Brazilian ideal, sympathetic to the country's 'white beaches,
its huge mountains – and its beautiful tanned women':*
Oscar Niemeyer, Kubitschek House, Pampulha, Minas Gerais, 1943

are a synthesis of local and international, historical and modern, concerns, the roofs evoking the double pitch of the monasteries and royal palaces of precolonial Kandy, while the interiors successfully combine Sinhalese, Buddhist and Western features. Not only do Bawa's buildings provide a home for the nation's legislative government, they also grant us a seductive image of what a modern Sri Lankan citizen might be like.

11.

There turned out to be a number of domestic buildings, in Tokyo and elsewhere, in subtle sympathy with the inner aspirations of the great traditional works of Japanese architecture.

The virtues of the nation's architecture – simplicity, efficiency, modesty, elegance – could be re-encountered in houses which to the casual eye seemed to have no contact with the past. Only on closer inspection did

'A house like me':
Geoffrey Bawa, Parliament Island, Colombo, 1982

one realise that a sensibility almost identical to that of ancient houses had been embedded in contemporary materials.

On a back street in Tokyo, one such house showed a blank concrete face to the world. A front door made of steel gave onto a narrow passage which in turn opened out into a whitewashed two-storey atrium, illuminated by diffused light that shone through frosted windows in the roof. Although this was a domestic space, it had a quality of emptiness and purity more typically associated with religious buildings. In inviting a retreat from the world, the house seemed to be honouring the Zen Buddhist belief in a need to create a refuge from daily life, not in order to forgo reality but so as more closely to approach certain of its central inner truths.

There were no windows with views in this house, perhaps the better to help its inhabitants see what truly needed to be observed. The light which washed down from above had the same gentle, indirect value as the glow

Tezuka Architects, Jyubako House, Setagaya-ku, Tokyo, 2004

emanating from a *shoji* screen. The architect had realised, as many of his lesser colleagues had not, that this luminous effect was in no way dependent on the use of paper and wood and could be achieved just as well, and in a more enduring manner, through panes of sandblasted glass. Thanks to these, the house had an otherworldly, abstracted air: to be inside it was to feel close to a realm of shadows and mist. When it rained, the pitter-patter of water sounded overhead, but the glass revealed nothing of the clouds from which the raindrops fell. This was an architecture designed to train the mind away from phenomena and towards essences.

In a second house, the two wings of the property were connected by an open atrium, so that even in winter it was necessary to walk outside in order to pass between the living and sleeping areas. While it did confirm a frequent Western complaint regarding the mysteriously glacial aspect of Japanese houses, this lack of insulation was evidently far from accidental, being tied instead to a desire, Zen in origin, to remind the occupants of their connection to, and dependence on, nature, and of the unity of all living things. A walk to the kitchen in midwinter delivered a brief and tart lesson about man's place in a larger and more powerful universe. Yet this wider natural world was evoked in the most abstract of ways, not through a view onto a lawn planted with mature specimens, but through the very temperature of the air, a thin carpeting of moss and the careful placement of three volcanic rocks.

These great modern houses I encountered were often simple in their furnishings, echoing the long-standing pull of Japanese aesthetics towards emptiness and austerity. The medieval courtier Kamo no Chomei, in his *Tale of the Ten Foot Square Hut* (1212), had described the liberation that awaits those who strip themselves of superfluous possessions and attend to the murmurings of their own souls. Simple wooden huts had as a result acquired a privileged place in the Japanese imagination. The great lords of the Momoyama (1573–1614) and Edo periods had every few months left their mansions and castles behind to spend time in huts, in obedience to the Zen insight that spiritual enlightenment can come only through a life without embellishment.

Others of these modern dwellings were just as faithful to the traditional Japanese fondness for material imperfection. The heavy outside walls of one weekend house a few hours' drive out of Tokyo were constructed from panels of rough and rusting iron, stained by moss and water. No attempt had been made to clean up these stains or to protect the material with a network of drainpipes; indeed, there seemed a deliberate joy to be had here in watching nature attack the works of man. The architects of the older tea houses had for much the same reason left their wood unvarnished, treasuring the ensuing patina and marks of age, which they saw as wise symbols of the passing of all things. In his *In Praise of Shadows* (1933) Junichiro Tanizaki attempted to explain why he and his countrymen found flaws so beautiful: 'We find it hard to be really at home with things that shine and glitter. The Westerner uses silver and steel and nickel tableware, and polishes it to a fine brilliance, but we object to the practice. While we do sometimes indeed use silver for teakettles, decanters, or sake cups, we prefer not to polish it. On the contrary we begin to enjoy it only when the lustre has worn off, when it has begun to take on a dark, smoky, patina.' Buddhist writings associated an intolerance for the imperfections of wood and stone with the failure to accept the inherently frustrating nature of existence. Unlike our own disappointments and decline, however, those represented in architectural materials were of an eminently graceful kind, for wood and stone, and now concrete and wood, age slowly and with dignity. They do not shatter hysterically like glass, or tear like paper, but discolour with a melancholy, noble air. The rusted and stained walls of the weekend house made for a most artful receptacle in which to entertain thoughts of decline and mortality.

12.

Successful modern reinterpretations of traditional architectural styles move us not only at an aesthetic level. They show us how we, too, might straddle eras and countries, holding on to our own precedents and regions while drawing on the modern and the universal.

The great modern houses are happy to admit to their youth and honestly to benefit from the advances of contemporary materials, but they also know how to respond to the appealing themes of their ancestry and can thereby heal the traumas generated by an era of brutally rapid change. Without patronising the history they profess to love, they show us how we, too, might carry the valuable parts of the past and the local into a restless global future.

13.

A few months after returning from Japan, I found myself on a road trip through Holland, and realised that the Dutch were on occasion as capable of pastiche as the Japanese. Here also were many houses that gave no clue as to how a fulfilled life might be lived in the present and therefore, while a great deal more coherent with their location than their brethren near Nagasaki, were no less incoherent with their era.

But on the road west from Amsterdam, on the way to Haarlem and the coast, I came across a new quarter of the village of Vijfhuizen, which triumphantly corrected all the errors of which the Huis Ten Bosch Dutch Village had been so guilty, for its houses had not only grown up in the appropriate country, they had also beautifully adapted themselves to the century in which they were built.

From a distance, the village looked traditional. The roofs were pitched, and the houses spaced out as on a typical suburban grid. Only on nearing the site did one start to notice particularly contemporary touches: the profiles of the buildings were sharply edged, as though suggesting a touch

Reconciling the old and new on a Swiss mountain:
Peter Zumthor, Gugalun House, Versam, 1994

of irony or self-consciousness about their primordial shapes. The roofs, instead of being tiled, were made of ribbed-steel plating, while the walls, rather than being made of brick, were a mixture of steel panels and identically grooved wood. In this combination of traditional form and modern materials, one sensed the unfolding of a mutually respectful conversation between past and present.

The houses knew how to accommodate themselves to the realities of the modern Netherlands while remaining quietly aware of their lineage. They looked like reinventions of the archetypal Dutch home that had succeeded in succumbing neither to nostalgia nor to amnesia.

Coherence in place and in time:
S333 Architects, New Quarter, Vijfhuizen, 2004

Self-knowledge

1.

I once spent a summer in a small hotel in the second arrondissement in Paris, a stone's throw away from the chilly seriousness of the old Bibliothèque Nationale, where I repaired every morning in a vain attempt to research a book I hoped to write (but never did). It was a lively part of town, and when I was bored with my work, which was most of the time, I would often sit in a café adjacent to my hotel named, as if out of a tourist guide, Chez Antoine. Antoine was dead, but his brother-in-law, Bertrand, had taken over the café and ran it with unusual conviviality and charisma. Everyone, it seemed, dropped by Chez Antoine at some point in the day. Elegant women would have coffee and a cigarette at the counter in the morning. Policemen lunched there, students whiled away the afternoons on the covered terrace, and by evening there'd be a mixture of scholars, politicians, prostitutes, divorcees and tourists, flirting, arguing, having dinner, smoking and playing pinball. As a result, although I was alone in Paris, and went for days hardly speaking to anyone, I felt none of the alienation with which I was familiar in other cities – in Los Angeles, for example, where I had once lived for a few weeks in a block between freeways. That summer, like many people before and since, I imagined no greater happiness than to be able to live in Paris for ever, pursuing a routine of going to the library, ambling the streets and watching the world from a corner table at Chez Antoine.

2.

I was therefore surprised to find out, some years later, while looking through an illustrated book on urban planning, that the very area in which I had stayed, including my hotel, the café, the local laundry, the newspaper shop, even the National Library, had all fallen within a zone

The future of a great city:
Le Corbusier, Plan 'Voisin' for Paris, 1922

which one of the most intelligent and influential architects of the twentieth century had wanted systematically to dynamite and replace with a great park punctuated at intervals with eighteen sixty-storey cruciform towers stretching up to the lower slopes of Montmartre.

The plan seemed so obviously demented that it intrigued me. I discovered photos of Le Corbusier leaning over his model, explaining it to a line of local councillors and businessmen. He had no tail or horns. He appeared intelligent and humane. Only after properly understanding how a rational person might come up with an idea to destroy half of central Paris, only after sympathising with the aspirations behind the plan and respecting its logic, did it seem fair to begin to mock, or indeed feel superior to, this remarkable conception of the future of a city.

3.

Le Corbusier had drawn up his Parisian scheme at a moment of un-equalled urban crisis. Across the developing world, cities were explo-ding in size. In 1800 the French capital was home to 647,000 people. By 1910 three million were squeezed within its inadequate confines. Much of France's peasant class had within a few years decided that it would collectively put down its scythes in order to head for the greater oppor-tunities of the city – unleashing an environmental and social catastrophe in the process.

Under the eaves of apartment buildings, several families typically shared a single room. In 1900, in the poorer districts of Paris, one toilet generally served seventy residents. A cold-water tap was a luxury. Factories and workshops were sited in the middle of residential areas, emitting smoke and deadly effluents. Children played in courtyards awash with raw sewage. Cholera and tuberculosis were a constant threat. Streets were choked by traffic day and night. Evening papers reported a steady stream of accidents involving severed limbs. Following a collision with an omnibus, a horse was impaled on a lamp-post on the Avenue de l'Opéra. There was not much that was picturesque about the early-twentieth-century city.

4.

Le Corbusier, for one, was horrified by such conditions. 'All cities have fallen into a state of anarchy,' he remarked. 'The world is sick.' Given the scale of the crisis, drastic measures were in order, and the architect was in no mood to feel sentimental about their side effects. Historic Paris was, after all, just a byword for tubercular Paris.

His manifesto, contained in two books, *The City of Tomorrow and Its Planning* (1925) and *The Radiant City* (1933), called for a dramatic break from the past: 'The existing centres must come down. To save itself every great city must rebuild its centre.' In order to alleviate overcrowding, the ancient low-rise buildings would have to be replaced by a new kind of structure only recently made possible by advances in reinforced concrete technology: the skyscraper. '2,700 people will use one front door,' marvelled Le Corbusier, who went on to imagine ever taller towers, some housing as many as 40,000 people. When he visited New York for the first time, he came away disappointed by the scale of the buildings. 'Your skyscrapers are too small,' he told a surprised journalist from the *Herald Tribune*.

By building upwards, two problems would be resolved at a stroke: overcrowding and urban sprawl. With room enough for everyone in towers, there would be no need for cities to spread outwards and devour the countryside in the process. 'We must eliminate the suburbs,' recommended Le Corbusier, whose objection was as much based on his hatred of what he took to be the narrow mental outlook of suburbanites as on the aesthetics of their picket-fenced villas. In the new kind of city, the plea-

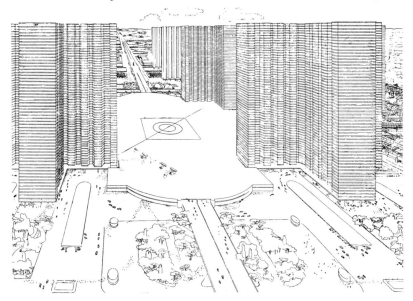

From Le Corbusier, *The City of Tomorrow and Its Planning*, 1925

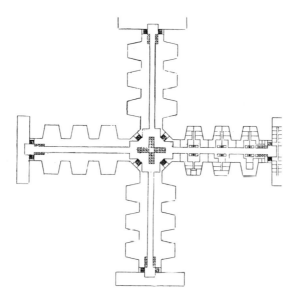

A skyscraper for 40,000 people:
From Le Corbusier, *The City of Tomorrow and Its Planning,* 1925

sures of the town would be available to all. Despite a population density of 1,000 per hectare, everyone would be comfortably housed. Even the concierge would have his own study, added Le Corbusier.

There would be ample green space as well, as up to 50 per cent of urban land would be devoted to parks – for, as the architect put it, 'the sports ground must be at the door of the house.' What was more, the new city would not merely have parks; it would itself be a vast park, with large towers dotted among the trees. On the roofs of the apartment blocks, there would be games of tennis, and sunbathing on the shores of artificial beaches.

Simultaneously, Le Corbusier planned to abolish the city street: 'Our streets no longer work. Streets are an obsolete notion. There ought not to be such things as streets; we have to create something that will replace them.' He witheringly pointed out that the design of Paris's street plan dated from the middle of the sixteenth century, when 'the only wheeled traffic consisted of

This crossroad
sents a fresh de
ment in the histc
mankind: death o
or at least a perm
threat of it.

Everything here is paradox and disorder: individual liberty
destroying collective liberty. Lack of discipline.

From Le Corbusier, *The Radiant City*, 1933

two vehicles, the Queen's coach and that of the Princess Diane.' He resented the fact that the legitimate demands of both cars and people were constantly and needlessly compromised, and he therefore recommended that the two henceforth be separated. In the new city, people would have footpaths all to themselves, winding through woods and forests ('No pedestrian will ever meet an automobile, ever!'), while cars would enjoy massive and dedicated motorways, with smooth, curving interchanges, thus guaranteeing that no driver would ever have to slow down for the sake of a pedestrian.

Even more than Paris, New York was for Le Corbusier the epitome of an illogical city, because it had managed to graft skyscrapers, the buildings of the future, onto a tight street plan better suited to a medieval settlement. On his trip around the United States, he advised his increasingly bemused American hosts that Manhattan ought to be demolished to make way for a fresh and more 'Cartesian' attempt at urban design.

The division of cars and people was but one element in Le Corbusier's plan for a thoroughgoing reorganisation of life in the new city. All functions would now be untangled. There would no longer be factories, for example, in the middle of residential areas, thus no more forging of iron while children were trying to sleep near by.

The new city would be an arena of green space, clean air, ample accommodation and flowers – and not just for the few but, as a caption in *The Radiant City* promised, 'for all of us!!!'

5.

Ironically, what Le Corbusier's dreams helped to generate were the dystopian housing estates that now ring historic Paris, the waste lands from which tourists avert their eyes in confused horror and disbelief on their way into the city. To take an overland train to the most violent and degraded of these places is to realise all that Le Corbusier forgot about architecture and, in a wider sense, about human nature.

For example, he forgot how tricky it is when just a few of one's 2,699 neighbours decide to throw a party or buy a handgun. He forgot how drab reinforced concrete can seem under a grey sky. He forgot how awkward it is when someone lights a fire in the lift and home is on the forty-fourth floor. He forgot, too, that while there is much to hate about slums, one thing we don't mind about them is their street plan. We appreciate buildings which form continuous lines around us and make us feel as safe in the open air as we do in a room. There is something enervating about a landscape neither predominantly free of buildings nor tightly compacted, but littered with towers distributed without respect for edges or lines, a landscape which denies us the true pleasures of both nature and urbanisation. And because such an environment is uncomfortable, there is always a greater risk that people will respond abusively to it, that they will come to the ragged patches of earth between their towers and urinate on tyres, burn cars, inject drugs – and express all the darkest sides of their nature against which the scenery can mount no protest.

In his haste to distinguish cars from pedestrians, Le Corbusier also lost sight of the curious codependence of these two apparently antithetical forces. He forgot that without pedestrians to slow them down, cars are apt to go too fast and kill their drivers, and that without the eyes of cars on them, pedestrians can feel vulnerable and isolated. We admire New York precisely because the traffic and crowds have been coerced into a difficult but fruitful alliance.

A city laid out on apparently rational grounds, where different specialised facilities (the houses, the shopping centre, the library) are separated from one another across a vast terrain connected by motorways, deprives its inhabitants of the pleasures of incidental discoveries and presupposes that we march from place to place with a sense of unflagging purpose. But whereas we may leave the house with the ostensible object of consulting a book in a library, we may nevertheless be delighted on the way by the sight of the fishmonger laying out his startled, bug-eyed catch on sheets of ice, by workmen hoisting patterned sofas into apartment blocks, by leaves opening their tender green palms to the spring sunshine, or by a girl with chestnut hair and glasses reading a book at the bus stop.

The addition of shops and offices adds a degree of excitement to otherwise inert, dormitory areas. Contact, even of the most casual kind, with commercial enterprises gives us a transfusion of an energy we are not always capable of producing ourselves. Waking up isolated and confused at three in the morning, we can look out of the window and draw solace from the blinking neon signs in a storefront across the road, advertising bottled beer or twenty-four-hour pizza and, in their peculiar way, evoking a comforting human presence through the paranoid early hours.

All of this, Le Corbusier forgot – as architects often will.

6.

Then again, omissions are to be expected given the difficulties of under-standing our needs and converting this knowledge into the unambiguous language of the architectural plan. It is easy enough to recognise when a room is properly lit and a staircase easy to navigate, but so much harder to convert this intuitive sense of well-being into a logical understanding of the reasons for it. To design means forcing ourselves to unlearn what we believe we already know, patiently to take apart the mechanisms behind our reflexes and to acknowledge the mystery and stupefying complexity of everyday gestures like switching off a light or turning on a tap.

No wonder so many buildings provide sad testimony to the arduous-ness of self-knowledge. No wonder there are so many rooms and cities where architects have failed to convert an unconscious grasp of their own needs into reliable instructions for satisfying the needs of others.

Our behaviour is riddled with eccentricities which frustrate casual attempts at prediction. Rather than sitting in the middle of a room on a soft armchair, we are capable of deciding that we feel more comfortable perched on a hard bench set against the walls. We may ignore the path built for us by a landscape architect in order to trace out our own shortcut – just as our children may find it more amusing to play around a car-park ventilation shaft than on a purpose-built playground.

Our designs go wrong because our feelings of contentment are woven from fine and unexpected filaments. It isn't sufficient that our chairs com-fortably support us; they should in addition afford us a sense that our backs are covered, as though we were at some level still warding off ancestral fears of attacks by a predator. When we approach front doors, we appreci-ate those that have a small threshold in front of them, a piece of railing, a canopy or a simple line of flowers or stones – features that help us to mark the transition between public and private space and appease the anxiety of entering or leaving a house.

We don't generally experience chronic pain when the fine-grained features of design have been ignored; we are simply forced to work harder to overcome confusion and eddies of unease. Yet if someone were to ask us what was the matter, we might not know how to elaborate on the malign features of our environment. We might resort to mystical language, citing unlucky harmonies between the sofa and the carpet, inauspicious magnetisms emanating from the door or contrary energies flowing out of the window – such terms compensating for the difficulties we otherwise have in explaining our irritations. Although nothing in our feeling about places can honestly be said to defy reason, it is not hard to see why we might look to a religious superstructure to lend substance to our elusive discomforts.

However, these can in the end always be traced back to nothing more occult than a failure of empathy, to architects who forgot to pay homage to the quirks of the human mind, who allowed themselves to be seduced by a simplistic vision of who we might be, rather than attending to the labyrinthine reality of who we are.

7.

The failure of architects to create congenial environments mirrors our inability to find happiness in other areas of our lives. Bad architecture is in the end as much a failure of psychology as of design. It is an example expressed through materials of the same tendency which in other domains will lead us to marry the wrong people, choose inappropriate jobs and book unsuccessful holidays: the tendency not to understand who we are and what will satisfy us.

In architecture, as in so much else, we cast around for explanations to our troubles and fix on platitudinous targets. We get angry when we should realise we are sad and tear down ancient streets when we ought instead to introduce proper sanitation and street lights. We learn the wrong lessons from our griefs while grasping in vain for the origins of contentment.

The places we call beautiful are, by contrast, the work of those rare architects with the humility to interrogate themselves adequately about their desires and the tenacity to translate their fleeting apprehensions of joy into logical plans – a combination that enables them to create environments that satisfy needs we never consciously knew we even had.

VI. The Promise of a Field

1.

A field somewhere outside a town. For a few million years, it slept under a blanket of ice. Then a group of people with pronounced lower jaws settled on it, lit their fires and, on a stone plinth, sacrificed an occasional animal to strange gods. Millennia went by. The plough was invented, and wheat and barley were sown. The monks owned the field, then the king, then a merchant, and in the end a farmer, who received a generous sum from the government in return for surrendering it to the colourful progress of meadow buttercups, ox-eye daisies and red clover.

The field has had an eventful life. A German bomber far off its target flew over it in the war. Children interrupted long car journeys to be sick on the edge of it. People lay down in it in the evenings and wondered whether the lights overhead were stars or satellites. Ornithologists tramped through it in oatmeal-coloured socks and spotted families of Black Redstarts. Two Norwegian couples on a bicycling tour of the British Isles camped here for a night and, in their tents, sang 'Anne Knutsdotter' and 'Mellom Bakkar og Berg'. Foxes looked around. Mice made exploratory journeys. Worms kept their heads down.

But time has run out for the field. The patch of dandelions will soon be the living room of number 24. A few metres away, among the corn poppies, will be the garage for number 25, and there, in the white campions, its dining room, where a person not yet born will one day have an argument with his or her parents. Above the hedgerow, there'll be a child's room, drawn up by a woman working on a computer in an airconditioned office in a business park near a motorway. A man in an airport on the other side of the world will miss his family and think of home, its foundations dug where a puddle now lies. Great Corsby Village will do its best to imply its age and inevitability, and nothing more will be said of the redstarts, picnics or the long summer's evening that rang to the sound of 'Mellom Bakkar og Berg'.

2.

The building of new houses is typically synonymous with desecration, with the birth of neighbourhoods less beautiful than the countryside they have replaced.

However bitter this equation, we conventionally accept it with passivity and resignation. Our acquiescence stems from the authority that buildings can acquire through the simple fact of their existence. Their mass and solidity, the lack of clues as to their origins, the difficulty and cost involved in removing them, lends them the unchallengeable conviction of an ugly cliff-face or hill.

We therefore refrain from raising of the tower block, the new antique village or the riverside mansion that most basic and incensed of political questions: 'Who did this?' Yet an investigation of the process by which buildings rise reveals that unfortunate cases can in the end always be attributed not to the hand of God, or to any immovable economic or political necessities, or to the entrenched wishes of purchasers, or to some new depths of human depravity, but to a pedestrian combination of low ambition, ignorance, greed and accident.

A development which spoils ten square miles of countryside will be the work of a few people neither particularly sinful nor malevolent. They may be called Derek or Malcolm, Hubert or Shigeru, they may love golf and animals, and yet, in a few weeks, they can put in motion plans which will substantially ruin a landscape for 300 years or more.

The same kind of banal thinking which in literature produces nothing worse than incoherent books and tedious plays can, when applied to architecture, leave wounds which will be visible from outer space. Bad architecture is a frozen mistake writ large. But it is only a mistake, and, despite the impressive amounts of scaffolding, concrete, noise, money and bluster which tend to accompany its appearance, it is no more deserving of our deference than a blunder in any other area of life. We should be as unintimidated by architectural mediocrity as we are by unjust laws or nonsensical arguments.

We should recover a sense of the malleability behind what is built. There is no predetermined script guiding the direction of bulldozers or cranes. While mourning the number of missed opportunities, we have no reason to abandon a belief in the ever-present possibility of moulding circumstances for the better.

3.

There was certainly no predetermined reason for parts of London to turn out as ugly as they have. In September 1666, after almost the whole of the city had burnt to the ground in the Great Fire, Christopher Wren presented Charles II with plans to rebuild the capital with boulevards and squares, perspectives and symmetrical avenues, as well as a coherent road system and an adequate riverfront. London might have had some of the grandeur of Paris and Rome; it might have been a great European city, rather than a sprawl which foreshadowed Los Angeles and Mexico City.

Charles II commended Wren on the beauty and intelligence of his scheme. But the decision about how to proceed was not solely his to take: lacking absolute power, he had to defer to the City Council, which was dominated by merchants anxious over their tax revenues and the difficulty of reconciling their competing property rights. Wren's ideas were evaluated by a team of commissioners appointed by the council and deemed too complex. Conservatism and fear took hold, and by February of the following year the plan was dead, Wren's boulevards having been consigned to fantasy and London itself abandoned to the interests of the merchants, who, loath to give up a sliver of their yearly profits, happily condemned the capital to three centuries and more of inferiority.

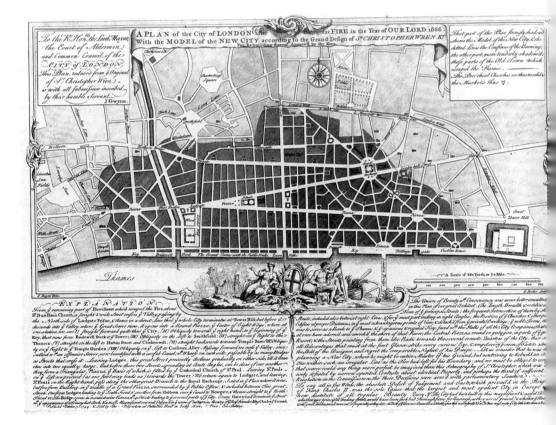

Christopher Wren, *A Plan of the City of London*, 1666

4.

The contingent nature of bad architecture is equally evident when we look at old maps of London's suburbs and see that what are now miles of blight were once acres of orchards and open meadows. There were farms at White City and apple trees at Willesden Junction. The terrain on which the disfigured forms of Shepherd's Bush and Harlesden stand today was at the outset an arena of pure possibility, on which streets rivalling those of Bath or Edinburgh might have been built.

The idea sounds pretentious only because we are reluctant to imagine that on a patch of ordinary ground where nothing significant ever occurred (aside from the slow gestation of generations of crab-apples), one of the great urban rooms of the world – another Royal Crescent or Charlotte Square – could be summoned to rise. We are prone to falling into a series of illogical assumptions which hold us back from being more demanding of architects: we presume that man-made beauty has been preordained to exist in certain parts of the world but not in others; that urban masterpieces are the work of people fundamentally different from, and greater than, ourselves; and that superior buildings must cost inordinately more than the uglier architecture which typically takes their place.

But, in truth, there was nothing especially promising about the hills of Bath before John Wood the Elder got to them, or about the fields near the swampy North Loch above the medieval core of Edinburgh before James Craig drew up his scheme for the New Town. Both were generic swaths of earth, furnished with grass, sheep, daisies, trees and, in Edinburgh's case, swarms of virulent mosquitoes. And, lest we feel tempted to shift our supposed locus of predetermined greatness from places to people, we should note that Wood and Craig, imaginative and highly persevering though they both were, did not possess a unique genius. The residential squares, gardens and avenues they built followed from principles which had been well known for generations. But each of these men was fired by the

The promise of Shepherd's Bush:
John Rocque, *A Survey of London and Country Ten Miles Around*, 1746

prospect of bringing a legendary city into being, a new Athens or Jerusalem, and in this ambition found the confidence to overcome the innumerable practical challenges involved in turning green fields into attractive streets. Having a belief in a special destiny, a sense of standing at a privileged moment in history, may well be grandiose and misguided, but it also provides an indispensable and therefore not unprofitable means of ensuring that beauty will have an opportunity to prevail.

Money can be no excuse either. Though Bath's crescents and Edinburgh's New Town were not cheap to build, we would be unfairly blaming a lack of inspiration on poverty by proposing that a tight budget ever condemned a building to ugliness – as a visit to the wealthy suburbs of Riyadh and the shopkeepers' houses of old Siena will rapidly and poignantly attest.

Fed up with hearing that no great cities could be built in the modern era because the necessary funds weren't available, Le Corbusier asked sarcastically: 'Do we not possess the means? Louis XIV made do with picks and shovels... Hausmann's equipment was also meagre; the shovel, the pick, the wagon, the trowel, the wheelbarrow, the simple tools of every race before the mechanical age.' Our cranes, diggers, quick-drying concrete and welding machines leave us with nothing to blame but our own incompetence.

5.

Ask the property development company what sort of houses will go up on the doomed field, and you'll be sent a waxy marketing brochure showing five different house types, each named after an English monarch. The Elizabeth II boasts chrome door handles and a stainless-steel oven; the George V has a fibreglass-beamed dining room and a Neo-Arts and Crafts roof; and the Henry VIII is, inevitably, a Neo-Tudor loyalist.

If, after browsing through the elegant presentation material, we still felt inclined to question the appearance of these buildings, the property developer would almost certainly retaliate with a familiar and apparently invincible argument: such houses have always sold rapidly and in great quantities. We would be sternly reminded that to scorn their designs would therefore be to ignore commercial logic and attempt to deny others a democratic right to their own tastes, bringing us into conflict with two of the great authoritative concepts of our civilisation, money and liberty.

But such a defence is not without its fault lines. A few of these came into focus as I flew to Japan, on my way to Huis Ten Bosch and the *ryokan*. Wedged in a window seat, unable to sleep, with the Arctic Circle shining a luminous green outside, I turned to a book entitled *The Pleasures of Japanese Literature* (1988) by the American scholar of Japan, Donald Keene.

Keene observed that the Japanese sense of beauty has long sharply differed from its Western counterpart: it has been dominated by a love of irregularity rather than symmetry, the impermanent rather than the eternal and the simple rather than the ornate. The reason owes nothing to climate or genetics, added Keene, but is the result of the actions of writers, painters and theorists, who have actively shaped the sense of beauty of their nation.

Contrary to the Romantic belief that we each settle naturally on a fitting idea of beauty, it seems that our visual and emotional faculties in fact need constant external guidance to help them decide what they should take note of and appreciate. 'Culture' is the word we have assigned to the force that assists us in identifying which of our many sensations we should focus on and apportion value to.

In medieval Japan, poets and Zen priests directed the Japanese towards aspects of the world to which Westerners have seldom publicly accorded more than negligible or casual attention: cherry blossoms, deformed pieces of pottery, raked gravel, moss, rain falling on leaves, autumn skies, roof tiles and unvarnished wood. A word emerged, *wabi*, of which no Western language, tellingly, has a direct equivalent, which identified beauty with unpretentious, simple, unfinished, transient things. There was *wabi* to be enjoyed in an evening spent alone in a cottage in the woods hearing the rain fall. There was *wabi* in old ill-matching sets of crockery, in plain buckets, in walls with blemishes, and in rough, weathered stones covered in moss and lichen. The most *wabi* colours were grey, black and brown.

To immerse ourselves in Japanese aesthetics and to nurture a sympathy for its atmosphere may help to prepare us for the day when, in a museum of ceramics, we encounter traditional tea bowls, for example, by the artist Hon'ami Koetsu. We won't believe, as we might have done without the legacy of 600 years of reflection on the appeal of *wabi*, that such pieces are puzzling blobs of unformed matter. We will have learnt to appreciate a beauty that we were not born seeing. And, in the process, we will puncture the simplistic notion, heavily promoted by purveyors of plastic mansions, that what a person currently finds beautiful should be taken as the limit of all that he or she can ever love.

In 1900 the Japanese novelist Natsume Soseki travelled to England and there noted, with some surprise, how few of the things he found beautiful stirred the locals: 'I was once laughed at because I invited someone for a snow-viewing. At another time I described how deeply the feelings of

The possibility of seeing beauty where we had not previously looked:
Hon'ami Koetsu (1558–1637), tea bowls

Japanese are affected by the moon, and my listeners were only puzzled... I was invited to Scotland to stay at a palatial house. One day, when the master and I took a walk in the garden, I noted that the paths between the rows of trees were all thickly covered with moss. I offered a compliment, saying that these paths had magnificently acquired a look of age. Whereupon my host replied that he soon intended to get a gardener to scrape all this moss away.'

There has, of course, always been the occasional Westerner who found beauty in rough bits of pottery or welcomed the appearance of a spread of moss. And yet it can be hard to champion such interests within a culture whose preferences run instead towards Palladian villas and Delft porcelain. We can be laughed into silence for attempting to speak in praise of phenomena which we lack the right words to describe. We may censor ourselves before others have the chance to do so. We may not even notice that we have extinguished our own curiosity, just as we may forget we had something to say until we find someone who is willing to hear it.

For all that we mock those who fake aesthetic enthusiasms in hopes of gaining respect, the opposite tendency is the more poignant, whereby we repress our true passions in order not to seem peculiar. We may stay quiet about our affection for daffodils, for instance, until a reading of Wordsworth endorses the sentiment, or suppress our fondness for ritualised, solemn snow-viewing until the merit of the practice is confirmed by Natsume Soseki.

It is books, poems and paintings which often give us the confidence to take seriously feelings in ourselves that we might otherwise never have thought to acknowledge. Oscar Wilde referred to this phenomenon when he quipped that there was no fog in London before Whistler started painting the Thames. Likewise, there must have been little beauty in old stones before Japanese priests and poets began writing about them.

The property developer's reflexive defence of existing tastes constitutes, at base, a denial that human beings can ever come to love anything they have not yet noticed. But even as it plays with the language of freedom, this assertion suppresses the truth that in order to choose properly, one must know what there is to choose from.

We should remember the lessons of the moss gardens and the pieces of rough pottery the next time we consider a reactionary housing estate. We should be free to imagine how much tastes could evolve if only new styles were placed before our eyes and new words in our vocabulary. An array of hitherto ignored materials and forms could reveal their qualities while the status quo would be prevented from coercively suggesting itself to be the natural and eternal order of things.

After being properly introduced to the true range of architecture, the prospective buyers of a red-brick, Neo-Tudor house might look beyond their original wish. A few might even surprise themselves by registering an interest in a raw *wabi*-looking concrete box, to whose virtues they had, through a journey of aesthetic education, been led to feel newly sensitive.

6.
Lest we begin to despair at the thought of how much might be required to bring about a genuine evolution in taste, we may remind ourselves how modest were the means by which previous aesthetic revolutions were accomplished.

A few buildings and a book have usually been sufficient to provide viable models for others to follow. Nietzsche observed that the development portentously known as the 'Italian Renaissance', which we might imagine to have been engineered by innumerable actors, was in fact the work of only about a hundred people, while the related innovation which textbooks call the 'rebirth of Classicism' depended on even fewer advocates: a single structure, Brunelleschi's Foundling Hospital, and one treatise, Leone Battista Alberti's *Ten Books on Architecture* (1452), were enough

Learning to recognise the charms of raw concrete:
Marte.Marte Architects, house, Voralberg, 1999

to impress a new sensibility on the world. It took just one volume, Colen Campbell's *Vitruvius Britannicus* (1715), to entrench the Palladian style in the English landscape, and a mere 200 or so pages of Le Corbusier's *Towards a New Architecture* (1923) to decide the appearance of much of the built environment of the twentieth century. Certain buildings – the Schröder House, the Farnsworth House, the California Case Study Houses – have had an impact quite out of proportion to their size or cost.

In all of these tectonic shifts, the tenacity of the prime movers was every bit as important as the resources at their disposal. The great architect–revolutionaries were a synthesis of the artistic and the practical. They knew how to draw and think, but also how to cajole, charm, bully, and play long, patient, careful games with their clients and with politicians. Because the days of absolutism are over (as Le Corbusier was not the first architect regretfully to observe), we can no longer behave like Louis XIV, who would only have to wave his hand for buildings to be moved as though they were children's blocks.

In a more collective, democratic era, architects have had to grow into artists of the committee meeting, people like Charles Holden who (together with Frank Pick) managed to persuade a British government instinctively opposed to serious architecture to make way for several masterpieces of station design on London's suburban underground lines. As Le Corbusier shrewdly observed: 'We must always remember that the fates of cities are decided in the Town Hall.'

7.

There are few harsher indictments against architecture than the sadness we feel at the arrival of bulldozers, for our grief is in almost all cases fuelled more by a distaste for what is to be built than by any hatred of the idea of development itself.

When bands of workmen arrived to sketch out the crescents of Bath

The architectural benefits of absolutism:
Engraving of Louis XIV ordering the building of Les Invalides in 1672 by R. Bonnard,
reproduced in Le Corbusier's *The City of Tomorrow and Its Planning*, 1925:
'He was able to say, "We wish it." Or "Such is our pleasure." '

or Edinburgh's New Town, as they cut their way through brambles and hammered measuring ropes into the earth, few tears would have been shed at the impending destruction. Although there were no doubt some old and noble trees standing on what would become residential streets, though there must have been burrows for foxes and nests for robins, these succumbed to the saw and the shovel with only passing sorrow from their previous denizens, for what was planned in their place was expected to provide more than adequate compensation. There was a fitting alternative to a field of daisies in St James's Square, there was beauty of a type to which even a tree could not aspire in Calton Hill, there was serenity such as no stream could match in the Royal Crescent. As William Morris pointed out, had we lived in Venice in her early days and watched the swamplands of the lagoon – muddy-beige smears of a kind still visible on the city's outskirts – being turned into streets and canals, 'as islet after islet was built upon, we should have grudged it but little.' Nor would we have been overly sad, Morris thought, to watch 'as Oxford crept north ward from its early home of Oseney… and the great Colleges and noble churches hid year by year more and more of the grass and flowers of Oxfordshire'.

We owe it to the fields that our houses will not be the inferiors of the virgin land they have replaced. We owe it to the worms and the trees that the buildings we cover them with will stand as promises of the highest and most intelligent kinds of happiness.

'As islet after islet was built upon, we should have grudged it but little':
The lagoons that ring Venice

Giovanni and Bartolomeo Buon, Ca' d'Oro, Venice, 1430

Acknowledgements

With special thanks to: Simon Prosser, Juliette Mitchell, Francesca Main, Helen Fraser, Tom Weldon, Steve Marking, Mary-Jane Gibson, Thomas Manss, Lisa Sjukur, Joana Niemeyer, Kelvin Murray, Miriam Gross, Dorothy Straight, Dan Frank, Nicole Aragi, Neil Crombie, Caroline Dawnay, Charlotte and Samuel.

Picture Acknowledgements

The author and publishers wish to thank the institutions and individuals who have kindly provided photographic materials for use in this book. In all cases, every effort has been made to contact the copyright holders, but should there be any errors or omissions the author and publishers would be pleased to insert the appropriate acknowledgement in any subsequent edition of this book.

All Le Corbusier drawings and photographs on the following pages are © FLC/ADAGP, Paris, and DACS, London 2006. **pp. 9, 55, 56, 57, 59, 60–61, 63r, 64, 66, 165, 240, 242, 243, 244**

p. 9 © FLC; **p. 14** © Digital Image Mies van der Rohe/Gift of the Arch / MOMA/Scala © DACS, London 2006; **p. 19** Balthazar Korab; **p. 21** Bayerisches Haupstaatsarchiv; **p. 23** Nigel Young/Foster and Partners; **p. 24** BPK, Berlin; **p. 27** courtesy of Bernhard Leitner from 'The Wittgenstein House' by Bernhard Leitner, Princeton Architectural Press, 2000; **pp. 30–31** Philippa Lewis/Edifice; **p. 32l** A.F. Kersting; **p. 32r** Gillian Darley/Edifice; **p. 33l** A.F. Kersting; **p. 33r** © Crown Copyright/NMR; **pp. 35, 36** A.F. Kersting; **p. 37** © www.visitrichmond.co.uk; **p. 38** A.F. Kersting; **pp. 40–41** Stapleton Collection; **p. 43t** © Crown Copyright/NMR;

p. 44 Irish Architectural Archive; p. 45 © NTPL/Matthew Antrobus; pp. 48–9 Institute of Civil Engineers; p. 50 Cameraphoto Arte, Venice; pp. 52–3 Foto Marburg; p. 54 A.F. Kersting; p. 59 © FLC; pp. 60–61, 63r © FLC; p. 63l Alain de Botton; p. 64 DaimlerChrysler Classic, Corporate Archives; p. 66 © FLC; p. 69t Bauhaus Archive; p. 69c Bridgeman Art Library; p. 69b Christie's Images; p. 70 Palladium Photodesign, Barbara Burg/Oliver Shuh; p. 71l Margherita Spiluttini; p. 71r Jean Nouvel; p. 72l Porcelain Museum, Porsgrunn, Telemark; p. 72r Bridgeman Art Library/ Hermitage Museum; p. 74 Michael Shanly Homes; p. 75 © Nacasa & Partners; p. 77 Bernhard Leitner; p. 79 Henry Moore Foundation; p. 80tl Tate Gallery © ADAGP, Paris, and DACS, London 2006; p. 80tr Jasper Morrison Ltd; p. 80cl Barford Sculptures © photo John Riddy; p. 80cr Alain de Botton © DACS, London 2006; p. 80bl Waddington Galleries/ photo Prudence Cuming Associates © Donald Judd Foundation/Vaga, NY/DACS, London 2006; p. 80br Roland Halbe/Artur; p. 83 Sotheby's New York © Bowness, Hepworth Estate; p. 84br Christie's Images; p. 85tl Gillian Darley/Edifice; p. 85tr Hijjas Kasturi; p. 85bl Kate Gibson; p. 85br AKG Images; p. 86 Philip de Bay; p. 88bl Marc Newson/Ideal Standard; p. 88bc bristan.com; p. 88br tapshop.co.uk; p. 89b Christie's Images; p. 91l Alinari; p. 91r Foto Marburg; p. 92t RIBA; p. 92b Heinrich Heidersberger/Artur; p. 94r © Gordon Beal/O & M Ungers; p. 95tl Martin Charles; p. 95tr Johner, Photonica/Getty Images; p. 95bl A.F. Kersting; p. 95br © Crown Copyright/NMR; p. 99 Philippa Lewis/ Edifice; pp. 102–3 James Morris; p. 105 Bernhard Leitner; p. 110l Alain de Botton; p. 110r © Jarrold Publishing and Westminster Cathedral, reproduced by permission of the publisher; p. 111 Scala; p. 113 Atelier Michel Jolyot; p. 115t AKG Images/Gérard Degeorge; p. 115b Werner Forman Archive; p. 116 Alain de Botton; p. 120 Agence Ingalill Snitt; p. 122 Scottish National Galleries of Art; p. 124 Fortean Picture Library; p. 125 Lucinda Lambton/Arcaid; pp. 127, 128–9, 130 Cameraphoto Arte,

Venezia; **p. 133** A.F. Kersting; **p. 134** Henning Marks/Edifice; **p. 138** Roy. George@Goddess-Athena.org; **p. 139** BPK Berlin; **p. 141l** Museum of Finnish Architecture; **p. 141r** Christian Richter; **p. 142** Tony Morrison/ South American Pictures; **p. 143** © J. Paul Getty Trust. Used with permission. Julius Shulman Photography Archive, Research Library at the Getty Research Institute; **p. 145** Dr Petra-Liebl Osborne; **pp. 146–7** John Heseltine; **p. 148** Permission of the Trustees of the Wallace Collection; **p. 151** Courtauld Institute of Art; **p. 156tl** Werner Forman Archive; **p. 156tr** © Agnes Martin, courtesy PaceWildenstein, New York/Christie's Images; **p. 156b** Department of Antiquities, Cyprus; **p. 158t** Courtauld Institute of Art; **p. 158b** Filip Dujardin; **p. 161** Robert Harding Picture Library; **p. 162** Aargauer Kunsthaus, Aarau; **p. 165t** © FLC; **p. 165b** Photo Richard Weston; **p. 167l** Lyndon Douglas; **p. 167r** P. Kozlowski and T. Cron; **p. 169** Margherita Spiluttini; **p. 176–7** Jolly Hotel Lotti; **p. 179** Österreichische Nationalbibliothek © Master and Fellows of Trinity College, Cambridge; **p. 181t** Fritz von der Schulenburg/ Interior Archive; **p. 181b** RIBA; **p. 184** iStockphoto/Nancy Lou; **p. 186** Courtauld Institute of Art; **p. 187** Cameraphoto Arte Venezia; **p. 188l** David Foreman/iStockphoto; **p. 188c** Interior Archive; **p. 188r** Agence Ingalill Snitt; **p. 189** Christian Richter; **p. 190t** Ivar Hagendoorn; **p. 190b** J. Kaman/Travel-Images.com; **pp. 192–3** Krier Kohl Archives; **p. 194** Klaus Kinold; **p. 197** Norman McGrath; **p. 198** Margherita Spiluttini; **p. 200** Jan Bitter; **p. 201** Agence Ingalill Snitt; **p. 202** FBM Design; **p. 204** Ian Lawson; **p. 206l** Domenic Mischol/Andreas Kessler; **p. 206r** A.F. Kersting; **p. 207l** Alan Delaney/Hopkins Associates; **p. 207r** Santiago Calatrava; **p. 208l** Paul Rocheleau; **p. 208r** Václav Sedy; **p. 209l** Dennis Gilbert/View; **p. 209r** A.F. Kersting; **p. 210l** Alain de Botton; **p. 210r** Musée d'Orsay/Bridgeman Art Library; **p. 212** Courtauld Institute of Art; **p. 213r** Richard Weston; **p. 214** Alain de Botton; **p. 216** Courtauld Institute of Art; **p. 218l** Janos Kalmar; **p. 218r** Pino Guidolotti; **p. 220t**

Alain de Botton; **p. 220b** Huis Ten Bosch Co. Ltd; **p. 222** Monkeydave .com; **p. 223l** François Jordaan and Kelly Henderson http//japanfjordaan .net/; **p. 223r** Ribersute Co. Japan; **p. 225** Alain de Botton; **p. 226** François Jordaan and Kelly Henderson; **p. 227** Alain de Botton; **p. 228** Dennis Gilbert/View; **p. 230** © Marcel Gautherot/Instituto Moreira Salles Collection; **pp. 230–31** David Robson; **pp. 232–3** © photo Katsuhisa Kida/Takaharu and Yui Tezuka, Tezuka Architects; **p. 237** Shinkenchiku-Sha; **p. 238l** Janine Schrijver; **p. 238r** Jan Bitter; **p. 240** © FLC; **p. 251** Bernhard Leitner; **p. 252** Duncan P. Walker www .walker1890.co.uk; **pp. 256, 258** Guildhall Library, Corporation of London; **p. 261l** Fujita Museum of Art; **p. 261r** Mitsui Bunko Collection; **p. 264** Ignacio Martínez; **pp. 268, 269** Cameraphoto Arte Venice

Index

About the Author

Alain de Botton is the author of seven previous books, including *The Art of Travel, The Consolations of Philosophy, How Proust Can Change Your Life,* and *Status Anxiety.* He lives in London.

A Note on the Type

This book was set in Janson, an excellent example of the influential and sturdy Dutch types that prevailed in England up to the time William Caslon (1692–1766) developed his own incomparable designs from them.

Composed by North Market Street Graphics,
Lancaster, Pennsylvania
Printed and bound by R. R. Donnelley & Sons,
Harrisonburg, Virginia